THE WILES LECTURES GIVEN AT
THE QUEEN'S UNIVERSITY OF BELFAST

Religion, law, and the growth of
constitutional thought
1150-1650

Religion, law, and the growth of constitutional thought
1150-1650

BRIAN TIERNEY

CAMBRIDGE UNIVERSITY PRESS

Cambridge

London   New York   New Rochelle

Melbourne   Sydney

Published by the Press Syndicate of the University of Cambridge
The Pitt Building, Trumpington Street, Cambridge CB2 IRP
32 East 57th Street, New York, NY 10022, USA
296 Beaconsfield Parade, Middle Park, Melbourne 3206, Australia

First published 1982
Reprinted 1983

Printed in the United States of America

British Library Cataloguing in Publication Data
Tierney, Brian
Religion, law, and the growth of constitutional
thought 1150-1650.
1. Constitutional history, Medieval - Addresses,
essays, lectures
I. Title   II. Tierney, Brian
342'.029   JC101

ISBN 0 521 23495 6

Contents

For
John, Chris, Helen, Ann Jane
With Love

Preface

Every historian who gives the Wiles Lectures at The Queen's University of Belfast incurs many debts of gratitude. It is a pleasure to acknowledge some of mine. I would like to thank the Vice-Chancellor and Mrs Froggatt for their exceptionally kind hospitality. Professor W. L. Warren and the staff of the History Department helped in many ways to make my visit to Belfast a very pleasant experience. I am grateful to the National Endowment for the Humanities for a fellowship grant. Above all I must thank Mrs Janet Boyd, whose generosity has made the Wiles Lectures series possible, and the trustees of the Wiles endowment for their invitation to deliver the lectures in 1979.

The trustees also invite historians from other universities to attend the lectures. After each afternoon's talk the visitors join with interested local scholars to form a kind of seminar where the day's performance is criticized and discussed. To a medievalist it all seems very fitting. After the *lectura* comes the *disputatio* - often lively, sometimes strenuous, always joyous. I am grateful to my colleagues for all the friendly criticism that I received on these occasions.

One purpose of the Wiles Lectures is 'to encourage the extension of historical thinking into the realm of general ideas'. The occasion tempts a historian to emerge from his specialist studies to address some broader theme. As will be evident, I succumbed to temptation. At our evening 'seminars' the questions that arose again and again concerned the methodological problems inherent in any such enterprise, the difficulties involved in an attempt to pursue the history of constitutional ideas over long periods of time. Two sets of questions kept recurring. Is it a legitimate undertaking for a historian to trace remote origins of modern ideas? Can he do this without falling into naïve anachronisms? And again: How should a historian evaluate the interplay between ideas and events? Does the study of ideas have any relevance for understanding the actual development of institutions? Since such questions arose so often it may be helpful if I indicate at the outset my attitude toward them. In doing this I am prescinding from a considerable body of recent very abstract work on the philosophy of history. Metahistory is a fascinating subject in its own right, considered as a branch of epistemology or linguistics, but it has little to do with the activity of a simple working historian.

A more appropriate starting point is provided by some observations of Herbert Butterfield, the first Wiles lecturer. Butterfield long ago called attention to the follies of a 'whig' approach to the history of constitutional thought. The whig historian, he noted, reads present-day ideas into the past. He imagines that he has discovered 'a "root" or an "anticipation" of the twentieth century, when in reality he is in a world of different connotations altogether'. He discerns 'an obvious principle of progress' at work in history. At his most naïve he imagines that his heroes of the past were 'fighting to bring about our modern world'. As against all this, the true historian studies the past for the sake of the past. He tries to see life with the eyes of another century. In considering Reformation history, for instance, he will 'adopt the outlook of the sixteenth century upon itself'.[1]

All this is salutary advice. It would indeed be foolish to see modern constitutionalism as the endproduct of some ineluctable 'principle of progress'. Yet in one way I may seem to have transgressed Butterfield's canons. He insisted that a historian should emphasize the 'unlikenesses' between the ideas of different historical epochs. I have often called attention to similarities. In doing this I have been concerned not so much to trace 'influences' from generation to generation as to call attention to certain recurring patterns of constitutional thought and the problems a historian encounters in considering their origins and development.

To explain this approach further, we need to go a little beyond the points raised by Butterfield's critique. After all, the categories of subjective bias (studying the past for sake of the present) and simple objectivity (adopting the outlook of the past upon itself) do not define exhaustively the modes in which historical discussion is normally conducted. A historian must, of course, seek to understand the past for its own sake, on its own terms. A scholar who presumes to write about medieval canon lawyers ought to be confident that, if he were transported back to the twelfth century, he could enter into discourse with them, could have something to contribute to their debates from within their own world of thought. This is the beginning of historical wisdom. But it is only a beginning. Living in the past is an antiquary's game; a historian's task is to explain.

Evidently he will not achieve any meaningful explanation if he anachronistically attributes twentieth-century ideas to seventeenth-century thinkers or seventeenth-century ideas to people of the twelfth century. To interpret a whole tradition of thought, a scholar needs to understand sympathetically the various stages of its development 'from the inside', as it were, from within the thought world of a particular time and place;

---

[1] H. Butterfield, *The Whig Interpretation of History* (London, 1931), pp. 12, 27, 16, 28.

but he also needs to stand outside the tradition, perceiving connections and adaptations over long periods of time that the makers of the tradition themselves could not be aware of. A twelfth-century canonist naturally did not know that some of his ideas constituted an 'anticipation' of fifteenth-century conciliar theory; the conciliarists did not know that their ideas would be appropriated by political theorists of the seventeenth century; and the seventeenth-century writers had no conception of how their ideas would be adapted in twentieth-century constitutional thought. But a modern historian knows all these things. I am not suggesting that it is impossible for a scholar to 'bracket out' such knowledge in approaching the writers of any given historical epoch - only that to do so all the time would impoverish historical discourse.

Herbert Butterfield, needless to say, was not unaware of such considerations. He wrote discerningly on the complexities of historical causation and on what he called 'mutations of ideas'. The biological imagery is suggestive. Other writers have carried it further; ideas in a society have been compared to genes in an organism. In this view ideas are seen as shaping, controlling elements; but if we were to press the analogy in detail we should have to appeal to a theory of evolution like Lamarck's or, more precisely, like Piaget's [2] rather than to the pure natural selection of a Darwinian. Not only are useless ideas weeded out by natural selection (sometimes); also valuable ones are modified by the changing behavior of the societies in which they exist.

The characteristic problem in studying the history of ideas is that patterns of words (encoding patterns of ideas) often remain the same for centuries; but, as they are applied in different social and political contexts, they take on new meanings. [3] In this sphere one is often inclined to write, 'Plus c'est la même chose, plus ça change.' And yet the word-patterns do not entirely lose their original connotations. (So too a highly evolved animal retains vestigial traces of its remote ancestors.) A historian of ideas therefore has to deal not only with origins but with survivals and adaptations. Whether he chooses to emphasize similarities or differences will depend mainly on the theme he is pursuing. To take a simple instance: A twelfth-century lawyer (Alanus), arguing for the supremacy of pope over emperor, wrote, 'The church is one body and so it shall have only one head or it will be a monster.' A seventeenth-century political philosopher (Pufendorf), arguing that a civil ruler should be empowered to control church doctrine, wrote that, otherwise, 'the state would become a monster with two heads'. If one were writing, say, a history of the secularization of Western culture, the difference would be all-important. Language that was first used in connection with the church

---

[2] J. Piaget, *Behavior and Evolution* (New York, 1978).

[3] This is true, for instance, of word-patterns such as 'What touches all is to be approved by all' or 'The ruler is greater than individuals but less than the whole people.' Some adaptations of these phrases are discussed in the following chapters.

was later applied to the state. If one is concerned with patterns of constitutional thought the similarity may seem equally interesting. Each author was trying to articulate a concept of unitary sovereignty and each, as it happens, used the same imagery to express it. Naturally, the patterns of words and of ideas associated with them grow more complex as one moves from simple affirmations of sovereignty to intricate theories of limited government.

In referring to the changing behaviors of societies, I have already touched on the second main topic raised at the outset of this discussion, the relationship between ideas and institutions. Here we can be brief. Institutions and ideas are not like chickens and eggs; it makes even less sense to ask which came first. At any point where a historian cuts into the tissue of the past he finds theories and facts inextricably interwoven. To be sure, political man does not live by ideas alone. Ambitious persons seek power; greedy persons seek wealth; social classes develop divergent interests. And institutions are shaped by all the conflicts and compromises that ensue. But then again, as Otto Hintze observed, 'Man does not live by bread alone; he wants to have a good conscience when he pursues his vital interests.' Moreover, a statesman will find it useful to persuade others of his good conscience too; power can rarely be wielded effectively over long periods of time unless it is perceived by the community in which it is exercised as a form of legitimate authority, not as mere coercive force. In studying the history of constitutional ideas we explore the various ways in which power can be legitimized and so ordered as to maintain its legitimacy. There is always a limited number of options. The stock of ideas available helps to determine the kinds of institutional structure that can find acceptance in any community. Moreover, such ideas do not always grow imperceptibly out of existing social realities; sometimes they have exotic origins. If the legitimating principle in a society is a very simple one - it is usually some form of divine right - and if a polity remains unchanged over long periods of time, historical analysis may be irrelevant. But, by the seventeenth century, very complex structures of constitutional ideas had grown into existence in the Western world after centuries of significant change. These ideas did not pre-exist eternally as Platonic abstractions; they were not engendered suddenly out of nowhere in the crises of the seventeenth century; they have a history. Studying the history of ideas will not explain the whole story of Western constitutional development; but we shall never begin to understand the story if we wholly ignore such study.

The Wiles Lectures are printed here substantially as they were delivered. The first one is partly a reformulation of ideas that I have considered elsewhere; it seemed useful to include this material as a basis for the subsequent argument. Here and there I have expanded the discussion and, in doing so, have borrowed some sentences from previous papers.[4] But the material presented retains something of the informality of the spoken word and it displays the characteristic limitation of the lecture form, extreme selectivity in the topics and authors considered. (Obviously one could just as easily write a history of absolutism as a history of constitutionalism from the kinds of source material that are used.) I have tried only to suggest an approach to the subject and to investigate a few typical lines of thought. There is no attempt to present a generalized theory, purporting to explain how all constitutional systems 'must' evolve. In particular, the role attributed to ecclesiastical institutions is something specific to the medieval West. It is conceivable that other societies might eventually produce systems of thought and practice analogous to Western constitutionalism; but in that case I would expect them to develop differently, if only because the Western pattern already exists and is likely to influence future syntheses.

When speaking at Belfast I added to the general title of the lecture series a subtitle, 'From Gratian to Grotius'. It was intended to remind my listeners of the pioneering study by John Neville Figgis in which he discussed the period 'From Gerson to Grotius', and so to acknowledge my debt to this perceptive work. However, although the twelfth-century canonist Gratian provides an obvious starting point for my argument, in the seventeenth century Althusius and the thinkers of the English Civil War, more than Grotius, provide the most adequate syntheses of the ideas discussed. (Though in this field it is hard to know where to make an end at all. One authority on American colonial history suggested to me that what we really need is a book that could be called 'From Gratian to Madison'.) Although it seemed inappropriate to keep the original subtitle, I have retained an appreciation of Figgis's work as an introduction to the lectures.

B.T.

May 1981

---

[4]   These are 'Medieval Canon Law and Western Constitutionalism', *Catholic Historical Review*, 52 (1966); ' "Divided Sovereignty" at Constance', *Annuarium historiae conciliorum*, 7 (1975); 'Aristotle, Aquinas, and the Ideal State', *Proceedings of the Patristic, Medieval, and Renaissance Conference*, 1979 (Villanova Univ.); 'Religion and Western Constitutional Thought', Hanley Lecture for 1980 (Department of Religion, University of Manitoba). I am grateful for permission to include this material in the present work.

I

Introduction

The main themes of this little book can be summed up in a couple of sentences. First: It is impossible really to understand the growth of Western constitutional thought unless we consider constantly, side by side, ecclesiology and political theory, ideas about the church and ideas about the state. And, second: It is hardly possible to understand unless we consider the whole period from 1150 to 1650 as a single era of essentially continuous development.

These are not new or startling thoughts; but they are not quite universally taken for granted among modern scholars. A few historians still feel able to reconstruct the political theory of the fifteenth century without any reference to the great struggle over the constitution of the church which was taking place in that era,[1] and to argue that a doctrine of the constitutional state could emerge only when (and because) civic humanists turned their backs on the whole thought-world of the Middle Ages. I want to suggest on the contrary that the juridical culture of the twelfth century - the works of the Roman and canon lawyers, especially those of the canonists where religious and secular ideas most obviously intersected - formed a kind of seedbed from which grew the whole tangled forest of early modern constitutional thought.

Many older historians emphasized one or the other of my basic themes. The Carlyles, in their standard history of medieval political thought, observed that 'The Renaissance may or may not represent a really new beginning in philosophy and science, it did not do so in political ideas.' But on the next page they added that relations between political and religious authorities 'did not in any significant way affect the development of the general political ideas of the Middle Ages'.[2] On the other hand, great social historians like Weber and Tawney saw that the interaction of religious and secular ideas was all-important in the formation of Western ideologies, but they emphasized areas of thought where

[1] This is happily not true of the most recent general survey of early modern political theory, Quentin Skinner, *The Foundations of Modern Political Thought*, 2 vols. (Cambridge, 1978). Skinner's valuable work includes a good treatment of fifteenth-century ecclesiology.
[2] R. W. and A. J. Carlyle, *A History of Mediaeval Political Theory in the West*, 6 vols. (Edinburgh-London), 1903-36, V, 2-3.

(they held) the religious changes of the sixteenth century led to a sharp break with medieval tradition.

Perhaps the best introduction to our subject is to be found in the old work of J. N. Figgis, *Studies of Political Thought from Gerson to Grotius, 1414-1625*.[3] Figgis was concerned with precisely the topics we shall be pursuing - the relationship of ecclesiology to political theory, and the problems of continuity and discontinuity in the transition from medieval to modern thought. Indeed my theme is manageable at all only because we have this fine old classic work which explores very discerningly the interplay between ecclesiastical and secular constitutional thought from the fifteenth century to the seventeenth. My task will be largely to supply some connective tissue linking the world of the twelfth-century lawyers with that of the fifteenth-century constitutional theorists whom Figgis discussed.

Figgis was a Cambridge don of the early twentieth century, a disciple of Maitland and Mandell Creighton, much influenced also by Gierke. In his *Studies* he set out to explain the growth of a theory of the constitutional state in the early modern world. He considered two major topics: the emergence of autonomous national kingdoms from the universalist society of the Middle Ages, and the change in the idea of political authority itself, 'from a lordship into an association'. Figgis related both of these developments to the religious crises of the late medieval and early modern eras.

He began his book in the early fifteenth century, not because that was an era of dawning civic humanism, but because it was the age of the Great Schism in the church and of the conciliar movement that eventually ended the schism. The dispute began in 1378. First two, then three pontiffs emerged, each claiming to be the true pope. The nations of Europe divided their allegiances between the rival claimants; intricate diplomatic negotiations failed to end the conflict; it seemed that, barring a miracle, the schism might go on forever. In this desperate situation an argument was put forward asserting that a general council could judge and, if necessary, depose all three 'popes'. (The Gerson of Figgis's title was a principal exponent of this point of view.) A great volume of theoretical writing appeared asserting that ultimate authority in the church resided in the whole community, that a general council representing the community could depose an unjust ruler, even a pope, that the best form of government for the church was some form of mixed constitution. These ideas, moreover, were put into practice. A general council actually met at Constance in 1414, removed all three would-be popes and installed a new one, so ending the schism. But, after that one success, conciliarism of

---

[3]   Figgis's book, based on his Birkbeck Lectures of 1900, was originally published by Cambridge University Press in 1907. A revised edition appeared in 1916. This was reprinted as *Political Thought from Gerson to Grotius, 1414-1625. Seven Studies* (New York, 1960). References are given to this edition.

course failed to establish itself in Catholic ecclesiology. The writers of the Counter-Reformation turned more and more to doctrines of absolute papal monarchy.

It was Figgis's great insight to see that the ideas of the fifteenth-century conciliarists did not die away altogether, that they had a continuing afterlife in writings on secular constitutional theory. The conciliarists, he wrote, had formulated universal principles of politics that could be applied to any society. They had expressed the theory of limited monarchy 'in a way that enabled it to become classical'.[4] Their writings were often used by major political theorists of the sixteenth and seventeenth centuries who borrowed the ideas of the conciliarists on church government and used them in constructing theories of the state. Figgis also pointed out that religious issues remained of central importance for the development of constitutional thought all through the early modern period. Most obviously, the breakdown of universal papal authority after the onset of the Reformation facilitated the emergence of independent kingdoms and encouraged a new emphasis in some quarters on the divine right of kings. But the Reformation also created religious minorities - sometimes Catholics, more often Calvinists - who found themselves persecuted by monarchs of different religious persuasions, and this circumstance stimulated a renewal of constitutionalist thought; it led to frequent questioning of divine-right theories, and to affirmations of popular sovereignty and of rights of resistance to unjust rulers. Figgis was a man of true Christian piety himself but he occasionally viewed the whole situation with a certain detached realism. He observed, for instance - it was one of his sharper comments - 'The two religious bodies which have done most to secure the "rights of man" are those which really cared least about individual liberty . . . the Roman Catholic church and the Presbyterian.'[5] Figgis of course was an Anglican.

Still, he was only repeating here a position that one encounters often enough back in the seventeenth century, though then it was usually expressed with a different animus. The remark of James I is well known: 'Jesuits are nothing but Puritan-Papists.' The royalist, David Owen, discerned a 'Concord of Papists and Puritans . . . for the Coercion and Killing of Kings'. Similarly John Bramhall, Bishop of Derry and a future Archbishop of Armagh, wrote in 1643 that the doctrine of divine right had two principal enemies; and they were again the Jesuits and the Puritans. (Bramhall thought that the papist error began in the eighth century when a pope first authorized the deposition of a reigning monarch; as for the Puritans, their spiritual ancestors were the Pharisees of the New Testament who refused to recognize the kingship of Christ.) The similarities of thought among writers of very different religious convictions are not merely coincidental. In seventeenth-century writings we can find

[4] pp. 56, 63.
[5] p. 154.

Calvinist and Catholic political theorists quoting each other's works approvingly, relying on one another for authority in this particular sphere without any evident sense of embarrassment. I think they could do this only because they were all drawing on a common tradition of thought.

The roots of this common tradition probably lay deeper than Figgis supposed. In considering the problem of continuity between medieval and modern political theory he displayed an extreme ambivalence. In one mood Figgis wrote, 'No subject illustrates more luminously the unity of history than the record of political ideas'; but he also wrote that 'when all is said . . . there remains a great gulf fixed between medieval and modern thought'.[6] He held that Gerson and Cusanus 'are, though we do not know it, a part of our modern world', but also that 'we have been divided from them by a revolution'.[7] Figgis's pages are strewn with such *obiter dicta*; his book remains fascinating in part because it is so full of paradoxes.

On one point Figgis was quite clear. He discussed not only the influence of conciliar ideas but also their origins; and he was certain that the conciliar theorists were reacting against the whole previously accepted teaching of the medieval church. Their movement, he held, strove 'to turn into a tepid constitutionalism the Divine authority of a thousand years'.[8] Much of Figgis's uneasiness when he faced problems of historical periodization arose from the fact that he wanted to present the conciliarists as a link between medieval and modern ideas, but he could find no precedent for their doctrines in the earlier tradition of medieval ecclesiastical thought. Instead he saw in preceding church doctrine (expounded, as he noted, principally by the medieval canonists) an imposing vision of world-order based on total theocracy, a vision of 'a universal Church-state with power ultimately fixed in the Spiritual head, bounded by no territorial frontier'.[9] This 'Canonist theory of sovereignty' provided a model for later doctrines of royal absolutism, Figgis noted; but in such a world-picture there could be no room either for autonomous secular states or for theories of constitutional governement.

Figgis observed, however, that some pragmatic experimentation did occur in the sphere of secular institutions. (After all by 1400 England had a Parliament and France an Estates-General.) Figgis thought that, although the conciliarists ostensibly supported their theories with appeals to Aristotle and the Bible, they were really 'arguing from the precedent of constitutional States'.[10] On the basis of contemporary practices in the temporal sphere, they built up generalized theories of church

---

[6] pp. 3, 15.   [9] p. 71.
[7] pp. 3, 70.   [10] p. 55.
[8] p. 41.

government which later could be taken over and adapted by secular political theorists.

There is a difficulty in the argument at this point. Figgis never really explained how secular constitutionalism had emerged from his theocratic world order of the Middle Ages. Perhaps he thought that no explanation was needed. In the days of optimistic liberalism before the First World War many historians supposed that constitutional government was a kind of normal, natural end toward which human history inevitably progressed. For them, it was the survival of ancient absolutisms that constituted an exception, an anomaly calling for explanation.

If the question were asked why limited, representative government first arose in Western Europe a simple, obvious answer was at hand: Western representative institutions grew from a primitive heritage of Teutonic virtue and liberty. This view remained fashionable over a surprisingly long period of time. Even so great a historian as Stubbs found it entirely convincing. Explaining the origins of English constitutionalism, he wrote, 'The English nation is of distinctly Teutonic or German origin' and, 'Freedom was in the blood.'[11] Figgis too, repeating the platitudes of his age, could write happily and thoughtlessly about Germanic liberty. More reasonably, Figgis mentioned the contractual relationships of medieval feudalism as a source of later constitutional theory. Also he was by no means insensitive to the importance of Roman jurisprudence. Figgis's treatment of the medieval background was far from naïve; but the whole thrust of his argument required that 'political liberty and secular politics' could emerge only when the dominant, theocratic, canonistic ideology of the Middle Ages had been challenged by the religious upheavals of the fifteenth and sixteenth centuries. How could it happen then that 'constitutional States' were already conveniently at hand in 1400 to provide a model for conciliar theories of the church? I doubt that Figgis ever thought seriously about the problem or was aware that any problem existed that called for serious thought. Figgis saw a need to explain how sophisticated constitutional theories first came to be formulated; but he apparently took for granted the growth of constitutional practices.

Nowadays no historian could set out from such a premise. The emergence of new absolutisms in Europe after the First World War destroyed the liberal dream of inevitable progress toward free institutions.[12] The

[11] Three hundred years earlier John Hare wrote, in similar vein, 'There is no man that understands rightly what an Englishman is, but knows withal, that we are a member of the Teutonick nation.' He explained that the 'free born men from Germany' had brought liberty to the 'servile body of the West'. *St Edward's Ghost* (1647), in *Harleian Miscellany*, VI (London, 1810), 92.

[12] But as late as 1936 A. J. Carlyle could still write: 'The conception of the divine right of the monarch has happily ... disappeared, and the theory of the absolute sovereignty of the State only lingers on among politically uneducated people or societies.' *Political Theory*, VI, 2.

rise of National Socialism in particular made theories of innate Teutonic virtue, which had long been criticized, seem finally absurd. The American constitutional historian, C. H. McIlwain, reacted strongly against such ideas in a little work of synthesis, *Constitutionalism: Ancient and Modern*, published in 1940. ' "Racism" may be a convenient cloak for national aggression', he wrote, 'but it is a very inadequate explanation of national constitutional development.'[13] McIlwain re-emphasized the importance of Roman law in medieval political thought. This was a significant contribution; but McIlwain was still ignoring a whole religious dimension of medieval society. By this time, however, other scholars were beginning to insist on the significance of the medieval church as a major influence on the whole evolution of Western government. One thinks of scholars like Maud Clarke in England, Georges de Lagarde in France, Otto Hintze in Germany.

Despite the work of such scholars, down to the 1930s a kind of mental block existed which inhibited the formation of an adequate synthesis in this whole field of study. Everyone agreed that the church exercised a pervasive influence on all aspects of medieval life; everyone knew that constitutional forms of government grew into existence in the medieval world; but the canon law that regulated the life of the medieval church was widely regarded as an essentially absolutist system, 'a marvellous jurisprudence of spiritual despotism' (in the words of Hastings Rashdall). Figgis too observed that 'The claim of the Popes to exercise illimitable authority had been worked out logically by generations of canonists.'[14]

In recent years several studies exploring Figgis's thesis have appeared.[15] The results are interesting. It seems that Figgis was quite right about the influence of conciliar thought. But he was wrong about its origins. Conciliarism was not simply a reaction against a canonistic theory of absolute papal sovereignty. On the contrary, the main conciliar doctrines had already been formulated in canonistic glosses of the twelfth and thirteenth centuries (works that were not readily available to Figgis and that still remain for the most part unedited). Moreover the fifteenth-century conciliar thinkers knew these writings and cited them as major authorities. Recent research on the medieval canonists, especially on the generation of great lawyers who wrote in the days of Innocent III, around 1200 – Huguccio, Laurentius, Alanus, Ricardus Anglicus, Johannes Teutonicus – has shown that their thought was less monolithic than Figgis supposed. Some favored papal theocracy; others defended the independence of the secular power. Some supported a doctrine of universal empire; others acknowledged the autonomy of national kingdoms. The

[13] C. H. McIlwain, *Constitutionalism: Ancient and Modern* (Ithaca, 1940), p. 91.
[14] Figgis, p. 49.
[15] The contributions of Francis Oakley are particularly useful. See especially his articles, 'On the Road from Constance to 1688: the Political Thought of John Major and George Buchanan', *Journal of British Studies*, 2 (1962), 1-31, and 'Figgis, Constance, and the Divines of Paris', *American Historical Review*, 75 (1969-70), 368-86.

canonists wrote extensively on constitutional law, on the proper limits of lawfully constituted authority, on representation and consent. They discussed at length the deposition of unjust rulers. Moreover their work influenced the growth of the constitutional state - the point that Figgis never explained - from the twelfth century onward. It is mainly the new research in this area of legal studies that makes it possible for us to see an essential continuity in the growth of constitutional thought from the twelfth century to the seventeenth. We should not forget or neglect Figgis's insights about the conciliarists; but a fresh approach to the subject can best set out from a different starting point, from the works of the medieval canonists and the society that produced them.

II

Juridical foundations:
society, church, and law, 1150-1250

The growth of a distinctive medieval tradition of constitutional thought was a complicated, difficult process. That is not surprising. Western constitutionalism itself is an unusual phenomenon in the general history of human government. In the past, when primitive peoples emerged from tribalism to form a civilization and a state, they most commonly turned to theocratic absolutism as the only effective way of maintaining order and unity in a complex society - to the rule of a sacred monarch, a priest-king, a divine emperor. So too, during our present era, the new 'third-world' nations, which everywhere began with brave dreams of democracy, have almost everywhere found it necessary to accept some form of dictatorship in order to survive. The classical age provides examples of city-states that learned to practice self-government within the framework of a small-scale society; but the Greek cities were eventually assimilated into a Roman state that moved from avowed republicanism to military dictatorship to overt theocracy. Humans find it consoling to imagine that the order imposed by their rulers reflects a divine ordering of the universe; most of the time, as Bernard Shaw observed, 'The art of government is the organization of idolatry.' (The great advance of the twentieth century has been our discovery that it is possible to combine all the advantages of theocracy with all the conveniences of atheism.) I do not suggest that this is an inevitable outcome of human affairs - merely a statistical probability. The historical problem of how constitutional theories and practices could first emerge and persist is a fascinating one partly because the practical problem of whether constitutionalism can survive and expand in the modern world remains so delicately poised.

ASPECTS OF MEDIEVAL SOCIETY

In Western Europe, from the twelfth and thirteenth centuries onward, events took an unusual turn. Nations turned aside from anarchy without stumbling into absolutism and began to build structures of constitutional government - and structures of thought - some elements of which have persisted into the modern world. The perception by modern historians that new constitutional ideas were growing up (especially among the jurists) at the same time that new institutions of government were emerging helps to make the situation more understandable; we need not suppose that institutional development was taking place in an intellectual void. But the emergence of the new ideas themselves calls for some explanation. They were related to the whole configuration of medieval society, and in the final analysis nothing less than the whole configuration will serve to explain their development; but, since we are dealing with such an uncommon set of ideas, it seems reasonable that the first question we might ask is: What was unusual about the society?

The question leads us necessarily to the religious aspects of medieval civilization. For, after all, there was nothing very unusual about the early substructure of Teutonic folkways that scholars used to find so fascinating. Ancient notions of customary law and of popular participation in local assemblies did persist throughout the Middle Ages and did continue to influence medieval ways of thought. But such practices are in no way peculiar to the Germanic peoples of Western Europe. They are found in primitive societies in many parts of the world; and such societies, as we have said, do not normally evolve into constitutional states. It is the same with the later growth of medieval feudalism. We can find rather close analogues for Western feudal institutions in other parts of the world, especially in Japan, but feudal practices elsewhere did not lead on to the distinctive forms of experimentation in the art of government that occurred in the medieval West. One could hardly exaggerate the importance of feudal attitudes in stimulating local hostilities to centralizing absolutisms throughout our period; but the preconceptions of a feudal society, taken by themselves and carried to all their logical conclusions, do not lead on to a doctrine of the constitutional state simply because they lack the basic concepts of the state itself - ordered public authority, rational jurisprudence, legislation regarded as a deliberate product of reason and will. In any feudal society tensions between central and local authorities will exist, and such tensions have to be resolved if an effective centralized government is to emerge; but the usual solution is a sacral monarchy, not a constitutional state.

It is only when we turn to the religious aspects of medieval civilization that we find situations which are extremely abnormal by the standards of other societies. Otto Hintze saw the significance of this. In studying representative institutions, he wrote, 'one faces a phenomenon that is characteristic only of the Christian West'.[1] This remark seems to me true and important but by no means self-explanatory. Obviously, the different forms of Western Christianity have co-existed happily enough with a variety of absolutisms at different times and places. If things turned out differently in the Middle Ages, it could not have been simply because of

[1] O. Hintze, 'Weltgeschichtliche Bedingungen der Repräsentativverfassung', *Historische Zeitschrift*, 143 (1930), 1-47 (p. 4).

the presence of Christianity; rather we have to consider the exceptional role of the Christian church in the organization of medieval society. The most obviously distinctive feature of that society was an unusual duality of structure. In the first great struggle of medieval empire and papacy, the Investiture Contest of around 1100, neither side was able to make good its more extreme theocratic pretensions. From then onward a duality persisted. There was never just one structure of government, presided over by an unchallenged theocratic head, but always two structures, ecclesiastical and secular, always jealous of each other's authority, always preventing medieval society from congealing into a single monolithic theocracy. Ecclesiastical criticism diminished the aura of divine right surrounding kingship; royal power opposed the temporal claims of the papacy. Each hierarchy limited the authority of the other. It is not difficult to see that such a situation could be conducive to a growth of human freedom, and the fact has often been pointed out. Lord Acton long ago wrote, 'To that conflict of four hundred years we owe the rise of civil liberty.'

Moreover, internal tensions existed within each hierarchy. In the thirteenth century feudal barons resisted royal centralization in the secular world while feudally minded bishops resisted papal centralization in the ecclesiastical sphere. The barons had more real power, but the bishops had a whole ancient theology of the church to draw on in defending their position and so were able to give to their arguments a more sophisticated and enduring formulation.

If we were to ask now, in a merely negative sense, why medieval society did not develop into a simple, theocratic absolutism, it might be sufficient to point to these various tensions within it and leave the matter at that. But if we ask a more positive question - not merely why absolutism was avoided but how constitutional theories and practices grew into existence - another aspect of medieval church-state relations becomes important. The institutional structures that we have described as being often in conflict were also in a state of constant interaction, mutually influencing one another. Frequent interchanges of personnel occurred between the two spheres of government; a medieval king's 'clerks' were also 'clerics', often holders of ecclesiastical benefices. The career of Thomas Becket, alternating between service to king and church, was unusual only in its dénouement. This situation facilitated an exchange of ideas and practices between the two spheres. Kings were annointed like bishops, and popes were crowned like kings. Papal sovereignty was defined according to rules derived from civil law, and imperial elections were conducted according to rules derived from canon law. One could give endless such examples. The interchanges become especially important for constitutional thought when ideas concerning representation and consent are involved. Such ideas often emerged first in the academic writings of the medieval canonists; but the canonistic doctrines themselves grew from a fusion of secular and religious ideas, and trained canonists staffed the chanceries of kings as well as the bureaucracy of the church. (G. P. Cuttino once investigated the careers of 135 middle-ranking administrators in the government of King Edward I of England; he found that most of them had studied canon law.) In discussing the 'configuration' of medieval society there is one more complexity to be considered. Growing up within each hierarchy, ecclesiastical and secular, were innumerable new corporate groups - monasteries, cathedral chapters, collegiate churches, confraternities, universities, guilds, communes. Their growth was stimulated both by movements of reform in the church that emphasized the apostolic way of life, a life lived in common, as an ideal to be emulated, and by the commercial revival of the twelfth century, which encouraged craftsmen and merchants to band together for mutual support. Even in the earliest hard-to-trace origins of such groups we can find evidence of interplay between religious and secular institutions. Often bishops, as lords of cities, were in conflict with the newly emerging communes; but sometimes, it seems, the communes originally grew out of diocesan peace associations. In the little French town of Agde, according to Foreville, the canons of the cathedral church first formed themselves into a corporate body, and then the citizens created a commune modeled on the example of the chapter of canons. A typical medieval guild displayed a fusion of secular and religious functions that would be hard to parallel in any modern institution.

Medieval jurists wrote extensively about the various kinds of corporative association, using the Roman law term *universitas* as a generic word to describe them all. A modern social scientist has observed that all societies contain elements of hierarchy and of collegiality; and this is most obviously true of the medieval world. By the 1250s even the barons of England could think of themselves, not only as members of a feudal hierarchy, but as a corporate entity, the *universitas regni,* the corporate body of the realm. Virtually all the medieval thinkers I shall mention were accustomed to day-to-day participation in the life of corporate groups, either as masters in universities or as members of cathedral chapters or religious orders. The everyday reality exercised a pervasive influence on their ways of thinking about the structure of human societies in general, including political societies.

The aspects of medieval life that we have considered so far - the existence of two hierarchies of government, the tensions within each hierarchy, the growth of corporative associations - all these things help to explain the content of medieval constitutional thought; there can be no understanding of the thought without a knowledge of the society. But there is a limit to how far social analysis can take us even if we were to press the argument in much finer detail. When considering medieval culture we cannot in the end simply dissolve intellectual history into social history - we cannot treat the history of ideas as merely a subdivision of the history of society - if only because social reality was not the only source of medieval ideas.

In twelfth-century civilization there was a sort of double duality, not only a duality between church and state but, also, so to speak, a duality between past and present. Claude Lévi-Strauss, in his well-known inaugural lecture of 1960, distinguished between a 'synchronic' and a 'diachronic' approach to the study of societies; the first approach considers only present-day realities, the second explores the whole life of a society in time. Lévi-Strauss, I think, was using his technical language here to make a simple point; some societies display anomalous characteristics that can be explained only as atavisms. But medieval culture was more complex than this. We have to deal, not only with atavisms (though they existed abundantly), but also with conscious revivals of ancient thought - first Roman law, then Aristotelian philosophy. To use the current jargon for once, we might say that, if the synchronic aspect of medieval constitutional thought seems complex, that is because its diachronic structure is quite unusually intricate. Medieval intellectuals approached the problems of their society with ideas formed in the earlier, sophisticated civilizations of Greece and Rome. But they did not merely repeat those ideas, parrot-like. They blended the ancient ways of thought with their own Christian world-view; they used classical concepts to rethink the political experience of their own society; and in doing these things they created much of the substructure of later constitutional thought.

The 'political experience' of the Middle Ages included experience with church structures; and this, as we have seen, gave rise to complicated relationships. A fine Renaissance scholar, Garrett Mattingly, has observed that it is 'intelligible . . . that the medieval church should foreshadow and as it were recapitulate in advance the development of the modern state'.[2] The process is intelligible, but it is not easy to understand; and it would not be intelligible at all if we simply supposed that the medieval church somehow, mysteriously, spun constitutional theories out of its own inner Christian consciousness, and that the state then simply copied them as if by a duplicating operation. Rather there existed always the tension and interchange between the two spheres that I have mentioned. The church borrowed secular ideas just as the state borrowed ecclesiastical ones; the church had to become half a state before the state could become half a church. Moreover, some of the secular ideas that the church assimilated were not taken from the contemporary medieval world but from ancient classical civilization. It is these areas of interaction that we need to study - the interplay between religious and secular ideas and, more subtly, the interplay between medieval present and classical past - if we want to understand why the Western tradition of con-

---

[2] G. Mattingly, 'Introduction' to Figgis, *Political Thought from Gerson to Grotius*, p. xiii.

stitutional thought developed in its unique way, differently from that of China, say, or ancient Peru, or Japan, or the lands of Islam.

THE CANONISTS: RULER AND COMMUNITY

For the twelfth century these 'areas of interaction' can best be studied in the works of the church lawyers. The canonists of that age were elite intellectuals in a vigorous creative society. Their work as teachers, prelates, administrators touched the life of their world at many points; and, as Maitland wrote, 'in no other age since the classical days of Roman law had so large a part of the sum total of intellectual endeavour been devoted to jurisprudence'.

At the beginning of the twelfth century a great revival of Roman law reintroduced into the feudal world of the West, with its countless petty jurisdictions, the ideas of strong central government exercising broad powers of legislation and taxation for the public welfare. Then about 1140, perhaps inspired by the example of the Roman *Corpus Iuris,* the canonist Gratian produced an immensely influential collection of church law. His *Concord of Discordant Canons* (often known simply as the *Decretum*) sought to create an ordered synthesis out of the tangle of apparently conflicting laws and practices that had grown up in the church over the preceding thousand years. The very structure of the work, filled with dialectical tensions, authority pitted against authority, text against text, reflects all the tensions of the twelfth-century world that produced it. But the content of the book was not drawn mainly from contemporary sources. Gratian began rather finely by presenting as a principal foundation of all law the timeless principle that we should do unto others as we would have them do unto us. Then the *Decretum,* like a vast disordered archeological mound, presented side by side juristic materials from all the strata of the church's past - ancient councils, decrees of popes, writings of revered church fathers.

Soon a great literature of treatises and glosses grew up around Gratian's work. The style of these writings is aridly technical; but, at the highest level of their thought, the Decretists set themselves a great task - to provide an appropriate juridical formulation for the ancient theological doctrine of the church as a people of God, an ordered community of the faithful. The revived study of Roman law with its emphasis on centralized authority coincided with the new reflections on all the early Christian texts assembled in Gratian's *Decretum,* and both currents flowed together in canonistic writing. Moreover, the Decretists lived in a twelfth-century society still soaked in the preconceptions of customary law, a society that was inclined to see law, not simply as the command of a ruler, but as an outgrowth of the whole life of a people. These varied influences produced an unusual complexity in canonistic constitutional thought. Most cultures produce a theory of the divine right of the ruler;

twelfth-century canonists were equally interested in the divine right of the community.

The Decretists certainly were fascinated by the concept of papal sovereignty - Figgis was not mistaken about that. Adapting an ancient phrase of Pope Leo I, they commonly held that the pope was 'called to a plenitude of power', other prelates only 'to a part of the solicitude'. In developing this teaching further the canonists relied primarily on the Petrine texts of the New Testament, as one would expect; but to explain more concretely the powers that inhered in Peter's office they also turned to the language of Roman law. The Roman emperor was not bound by existing law or custom; he could make new law. To the canonists it seemed that there were many bad customs in the church that needed to be abolished and many new laws that needed to be made. Hence they eagerly seized on phrases like 'The Prince is not bound by the laws', or 'What has pleased the Prince has the force of law', and, applying them to the power of the pope, created a new doctrine of sovereignty from their fusion of scriptural exegesis with secular Roman jurisprudence.[3] Often the resultant theory was expressed in high-flown rhetoric, as in these phrases of a thirteenth-century commentator, interweaving in typical fashion the claims of Peter and of Caesar.

The pope is the successor of Peter and the vicar of Jesus Christ, holding the place on earth not of mere man but of God . . . whence he rules and judges all . . . the pope has the plenitude of power to which he is called . . . so long as he does not go against the faith he can say and do whatever he pleases in all things . . . No one can say to him 'Why do you do this?' . . . What pleases him has the force of law . . . he can abolish any law . . . he has no superior . . . he is set over all and he can be judged by no one.[4]

Such rhetoric, however, conveys only one side of the canonists' thought. Early Christian texts are filled with a sense of community. They tell of community meetings, community sharing, community participation in decisions, and above all they reflect a strong belief that the consensus of the Christian people indicates the guidance of the Holy Spirit at work in the church. (At the Council of Jerusalem the apostles and elders announced their decisions with the words, 'It has seemed good to the Holy Spirit and to us . . .') Whatever power prelates possessed in the early church, they possessed it on behalf of their communities and as representing their communities; and many elements of this early stratum of the church's life survived in the texts of Gratian's *Decretum*. Gratian quoted Cyprian's well-known phrase, 'The church is in the bishop and the bishop is in the church.' He also included in his work a very influen-

---

[3]   This theme is explored in more detail in Walter Ullmann, *Medieval Papalism* (London, 1949), and J. A. Watt, 'The Theory of Papal Monarchy in the Thirteenth Century: The Contribution of the Canonists', *Traditio* 20 (1964), 179-317. Watt refers to a 'principle of juristic supremacy clothed in garments taken from the wardrobe of Roman law' (p. 260).

[4]   Gulielmus Durandus, *Speculum iuris* (Venice, 1525), I.i, p. 51. Gulielmus gave elaborate citations to both Roman and canon law in support of these claims.

tial text of Augustine, 'When Peter received the keys he signified the church.' The canonists also often cited similar phrases of Augustine, stating that Peter 'bore the person of the church' or stood 'as a symbol of the church [*in figura ecclesiae*]'.

Such language was inherently ambiguous, and the Decretists explored all its possible implications. When they wrote of the church's government they often suggested that Peter 'signified' the church in the sense that he epitomized all ruling authority in himself. But when they wrote of the church's faith they always interpreted the word in a disjunctive sense, as implying a distinction between Peter, a mere erring mortal, and the universal church understood as the whole Christian community, whose faith could never become extinct.[5] Even when they considered Christ's words addressed directly to Peter, 'I have prayed for you Peter that your faith shall not fail', the canonists interpreted them as a prayer for the faith of the universal church, not for Peter as an individual. We can illustrate this attitude from Huguccio, the greatest commentator on Gratian's *Decretum*, writing in the 1180s:

Vices and mortal sin shall never prevail so that there are no good persons in the church, whence Christ said to Peter as a symbol of the church, 'I have prayed for you Peter that your faith shall not fail.'[6]

And again:

Although the Roman pope has sometimes erred this does not mean that the Roman church has, which is understood to be not he alone but all the faithful, for the church is the aggregate of the faithful; if it does not exist at Rome it exists in the regions of Gaul, or wherever the faithful are . . . for it was said to Peter and in the person of Peter to the universal church 'that your faith shall not fail'.[7]

Similar passages occur in the works of many canonists writing around 1200.

In Decretist thought, then, we find both a strong emphasis on the sovereignty of the pope and a strong emphasis on the indefectibility of the community. The Decretists were not able to keep the two doctrines in separate compartments of their thought because of a practical problem implicit in the texts just cited. Medieval canonists did not attribute either impeccability or infallibility to the popes. They conceded enormous powers to the papal office, but they knew that the man who occupied that office was after all but a man. He had free will; he could choose to sin; he might err. A pope might even use all his great power to injure the

---

[5] Most of the canonistic texts given in translation here are from works that remain unedited. Unless otherwise noted the Latin texts are printed in my *Foundations of the Conciliar Theory* (Cambridge, 1955), *Origins of Papal Infallibility* (Leiden, 1972), or 'Pope and Council: Some New Decretist Texts', *Mediaeval Studies*, 19 (1957), 197-218 (cited subsequently as *Foundations, Origins,* 'Pope and Council'). On Peter as 'figuring' the church see *Foundations,* p. 35 n. 1. Even in the litany of papal praises given by Gulielmus Durandus, the author included the words, 'So long as he does not go against the faith . . .'

[6] *Summa ad Dist.* 19 c.7 (*Origins,* p. 35 n. 1).

[7] *Summa ad* C.24 q.1 c.9 (*Origins,* p. 37 n. 1). Other similar passages are presented in *Foundations,* pp. 41-5.

church. A glossator of Gratian's *Decretum* could hardly evade the issue because the *Decretum* itself recorded several stories of allegedly wicked popes of the past. This had a sobering effect on the canonists. One of Gratian's texts declared that the popes were to be presumed holy; the Ordinary Gloss of Johannes Teutonicus (*c*. 1216) observed, 'Note, it does not say they are holy but that they are to be presumed holy . . . which means until the contrary becomes apparent.'[8] Huguccio explained in rather lurid detail the kind of problem that could arise. A pope might become a heretic, or he might commit sins almost as intolerable as heresy:

> What then? Look! The pope steals publicly, he fornicates publicly, he keeps a concubine publicly, he has intercourse with her publicly in a church, near the altar or on it, and he will not stop when admonished . . . Shall he not be accused, shall he not be condemned?[9]

Since the pope of the time was the aged and respectable Clement III, all this was highly imaginative; but the canonists always considered the rule of an aberrant pope to be at least a theoretical possibility.

They were faced then with a central problem of constitutional thought. How could one affirm simultaneously the overriding right of a sovereign to rule and the overriding claim of a community to defend itself against abuses of power? If the pope was supreme judge, who could question his judgments? Who could condemn him? The Decretists' approach to such questions was to seek in the consensus of the unfailing church, expressed in the statutes of general councils, norms of faith and order that could bind even a pope. They were trying to set up a framework of fundamental law which so defined the very nature and structure of the church that any licit ecclesiastical authority, even papal authority, had to be exercised within that framework. A text of Pope Gregory the Great, incorporated into the *Decretum,* provided a juridical basis for this development. Gregory asserted that the canons of the early general councils were always to be preserved inviolate because they were established by universal consent (*universali consensu*). He added that anyone who went against the canons 'destroyed himself and not them'.[10]

Some of the earliest commentators on the *Decretum* raised the question whether this principle applied also to the pope. One problem was that the councils had enacted many minor disciplinary decrees (where the pope could certainly grant dispensations) as well as defining permanent truths of faith. The French *Summa Parisiensis* (*c*. 1160) accordingly declared that the inviolable canons of general councils were those that pertained especially to the faith.[11] About the same time Rufinus, in Bologna, declared that popes were bound by 'those statutes of the

---

[8] *Decretum Gratiani . . . una cum glossis* (Venice, 1600), Gloss *ad Dist.* 40 c.1.*
[9] *Summa ad Dist.* 40 c.6 (*Foundations*, p. 249).
[10] *Dist.* 15 c.2.
[11] T. P. McLaughlin (ed.), *The Summa Parisiensis on the Decretum Gratiani* (Toronto, 1952), p. 230.

ancient and venerable fathers promulgated with full authority to preserve the state of all the churches'.[12] Later writers conflated the two doctrines; by around 1200 they commonly asserted that a pope was bound by general councils 'in matters touching the faith and the general state of the church'.[13] A little later the parallel phrase 'state of the realm' appears in secular documents, and eventually Bodin will write of the fundamental laws touching the state of the realm that bound even his sovereign.

The canonists were able to reconcile this doctrine of conciliar authority with their teaching on papal sovereignty because, for them, the pope was an intrinsic part of a general council. The pope was indeed the sovereign head of the church in that no individual prelate was superior to him or equal. But the papal will could be expressed in different forms, through different channels; and, the canonists were coming to teach, it was expressed in its highest form when the pope acted in concert with the whole church, represented in a council. Johannes Teutonicus wrote, with deceptive simplicity, 'Where matters of faith are concerned a council is greater than a pope';[14] but he probably meant only that the pope acting with a council was greater than a pope alone. An English Decretist put the point explicitly: 'The authority of a pope with a council is greater than without.'[15] One is reminded of the later secular doctrine of the supremacy of king-in-parliament.[16]

So far so good. Standards of faith and order existed that the pope was not permitted to violate. But what if he did? In exploring this question the canonists anticipated almost every twist and turn of later resistance theory. The most radical view held that, in such a dire emergency, the cardinals or bishops in council held an authority superior to that of the erring pope and so could judge him. Thus Alanus wrote, 'It is true that a pope can be judged against his will only for heresy . . . this is so because in matters which pertain to the faith he is less than the college of cardinals or a general council of bishops.'[17] But this view was hard to reconcile with the generally accepted doctrine of papal supremacy.

Other canonists, starting from the view that the pope-and-council together were greater than the pope alone, argued that, if a general council had condemned a heresy and excommunicated in advance anyone who fell into it, then a pope who did so fall would automatically incur the sentence already pronounced beforehand. This view is found, for instance, in the French *Summa Et est sciendum* (*c.* 1185).[18]

Huguccio presented yet another position. Although he insisted that

---

[12] H. Singer (ed.), *Die Summa Decretorum des Magister Rufinus* (Paderborn, 1902), p. 13.

[13] 'Pope and Council', pp. 210-12.

[14] Gloss *ad Dist.* 40 c.6.

[15] Caius College, Cambridge MS 676, Gloss *ad* C.24 q.1 c.1, cited by J. A. Watt, 'The Early Medieval Canonists and the Formation of Conciliar Theory', *Irish Theological Quarterly*, 24 (1957), 13-31 (p. 28).

[16] As James Whitelock put it, addressing the House of Commons in 1610, 'the power of the king in parliament is greater than his power out of parliament'.

[17] Gloss *ad Dist.* 40 c.6 (Watt, p. 30).

[18] *Summa ad Dist.* 40 c.6 ('Pope and Council', p. 215).

only the whole church was indefectible in faith he was reluctant to concede that the pope could have any superior in the order of jurisdiction. Accordingly, he held that a pope who publicly announced his adherence to a known heresy simply ceased to be a pope because 'a heretic is less than any Catholic'. Huguccio also thought that the same principle applied if the pope persisted in notorious sin after due admonition, since then the pope seemed to deny the truth of the moral doctrine that he violated. A pope could not claim immunity in such cases because, if this were permitted, 'the whole church would be endangered and the general state of the church confounded'.[19] Huguccio's doctrine was carefully balanced. The welfare of the church was defended; but papal sovereignty was upheld too. Huguccio would never countenance any kind of judicial proceedings against a man presumed to be pope; an occupant of the papal see was to be removed only when his guilt and consequent self-deposition could be taken for granted.

Huguccio's position was internally consistent but it raised many practical difficulties. To mention only one: If there could be no formal trial of a pope and if a heretic was 'less than any catholic' then it might seem that any Catholic ruler could take action against a pope whom he chose to regard as evidently heretical. Again, Huguccio's doctrine held that a pope could be deposed without any formal procedure to establish his guilt; but, as the author of the *Summa Et est sciendum* observed, 'A man is not held guilty when he is accused but when he is convicted of a crime.'[20]

The *Summa Duacensis* (*c.* 1200) suggested a way out of the difficulty. The author, rather an extreme papalist, expressly rejected the doctrine that would later be called 'divided sovereignty'. 'We do not accept the opinion of those who attribute apostolic jurisdiction partly to the supreme pontiff and partly to the sacred college of cardinals or the whole church', he wrote. For this author jurisdiction inhered in the pope alone. Quite consistently therefore he maintained that the pope could not be accused of any ordinary crime since he could not be judged by his subjects. There remained the possibility of obdurate heresy. Here again the author maintained that no juridical superior existed who could pass sentence on a pope. But he held that the church could consider such a case 'not judicially but deliberatively'. And if the deliberation led to a conclusion that the pope's teaching was indeed heretical (and he persisted in it), then he automatically forfeited the papacy, *ipso iure*, by the law itself. A man could not be simultaneously a heretic and a pope.[21]

Once again this canonistic doctrine had many echoes in later constitutional thought. Centuries later, for instance, Pufendorf also opposed theories of divided sovereignty and defended the principle that a ruler

[19]   *Summa ad Dist.* 40 c.6 (*Foundations*, p. 249).
[20]   *Summa ad Dist.* 40 c.6 ('Pope and Council', p. 215).
[21]   *Summa ad Dist.* 40 c.6 ('Pope and Council', p. 217).

could not be judged by his subjects. He conceded that if a sovereign bound by fundamental law violated the rules that defined his office, he would forfeit his position in the very act of doing so; but Pufendorf also explained that 'an Act of the People, whereby they take notice of the Prince's Miscarriage and Forfeiture, doth not carry in it the Semblance of a judicial Proceeding'. Rather such an act was 'no more than a bare Declaration'. The idea that a community could formally take cognizance of a ruler's default without enacting a judicial sentence against him remained important both in theory and in practice.[22] Still more important though was the group of Decretist theories that sought to explain how, in some subtle fashion, supreme jurisdiction could inhere simultaneously in both pope and council. To understand these theories more fully we must first consider some other aspects of canonistic thought.

CORPORATION LAW: MACROCOSM AND MICROCOSM

Medieval canonists influenced the subsequent growth of constitutional ideas in two ways. The first way was through their overt arguments about the relationship between ruler and community (arguments that were often taken up at the end of the Middle Ages by the fifteenth-century conciliarists); the second way was through their reflections on the technicalities of corporation law. The Decretists not only explained the doctrine of papal headship in terms of the Roman law of sovereignty; they also explained the collegial structure of the church in terms of the Roman law of corporations. Here again we find an interplay of secular and ecclesiastical thought in their work.

Legally a corporation (*universitas*) was conceived of as a group that possessed a juridical personality distinct from that of its particular members. A debt owed by a corporation was not owed by the members as individuals; an expression of the will of a corporation did not require the assent of each separate member but only of a majority. A corporation did not have to die; it remained the same legal entity even though the persons of the members changed. In a famous phrase of the thirteenth-century canonists a corporation was described as a 'fictitious person'. Such a concept, it proved, could be used to define many types of ecclesial and political community.

The canonistic development of these ideas can be considered on different levels which we might call macrocosmic and microcosmic. On the macrocosmic level we encounter texts that refer to the whole church or a whole political commonwealth as a single body (*corpus*). But such usages did not necessarily have any technical significance; the word *corpus*

---

[22] Pufendorf, *On the Law of Nature and Nations,* trans. Basil Kennett (London, 1729), p. 698. At about the same time, many English Tories, who would never admit that any earthly power could depose King James II, reconciled themselves to the situation after 1688 by embracing the fiction that James had abdicated the throne by his very actions and that parliament had merely acknowledged the fact.

could be used in a general sense to describe any collection of individuals (as in our English usage, 'a body of people'). *Corpus* had a more specific theological meaning in ecclesiology, however, for St Paul had referred to the whole church as the body of Christ. During the twelfth century it became usual to describe the church as a 'mystical body' (as distinct from the 'true body' of Christ in the Eucharist) and in mid thirteenth century the ecclesiastical term seeped into secular usage. From about 1250 onward we can read of the 'mystical body of the commonwealth' (*corpus mysticum reipublicae*). Still, when such terminology was explored in detail, it usually led on merely to elaborate anthropomorphic conceits; the language took on a new dimension only when it was used in such a way as to apply to the whole church or commonwealth the technical concepts of corporation law.

This development occurred almost imperceptibly in the writings of the canonists. Around 1200 they began to discern that the legal concept of a corporation could define the structure, not only of small groups within the church, but of the universal church itself and of a general council representing the church. The issue arose first in discussions of the church's indefectibility. Usually, when the canonists wrote that the church's faith could never fail they meant only that, whatever calamities or defections might occur, the faith would always live on, if only in a few scattered individuals. (Thus, as we saw, Huguccio wrote that there would always be some good persons in the church.) But the doctrine of indefectibility could also mean that the church as a whole would always adhere to the true faith when it acted together, as a corporate entity. This approach was suggested by the author of the *Summa Omnis qui iuste* (*c.* 1186), who wrote that the church had never erred 'in its whole body'. This might still be taken as only an echo of Pauline teaching on the church as the body of Christ; but the author at once added, rather cryptically, 'Here is an argument that something is not understood to be done that is not done by the whole *universitas*.'[23] Another anonymous canonist used these same words and then added a reference to *Distinctio* 21 of the *Decretum*, a text that referred to Christ's prayer for Peter's faith.[24] (The author interpreted this, in the usual fashion, as a prayer for the faith of the whole church.) Finally Laurentius (*c.* 1210) brought the discussion to a conclusion by specifically linking the theological doctrine of indefectibility with the Roman law of corporations.

> That is not said to be done by the church which is not done by the corporate body itself [*ipsa universitate*] as in the Digest, *De regulis iuris, Aliud* [*Dig.* 50.17.121] . . . but although the pope errs . . . the Roman and apostolic church, which is the congregation of Catholics, does not.[25]

Dig. 50.17.121 stated the principle, 'What is done publicly by a majority is held to be done by all.' Medieval Roman lawyers, commenting on this,

---

[23] *Summa ad* C.24 q.1 c.9 ('Pope and Council', p. 213).
[24] Wolfenbüttel (Helmst. 33), Gloss *ad* C.24 q.1 c.9 (*Foundations*, p. 43).
[25] Gloss *ad* C.24 q.1 c.9 (*Foundations*, p. 46).

noted that the inhabitants of a city were bound, not only by a majority of all citizens, but also by a decision of a corporate body acting on their behalf. The canonists developed a similar doctrine concerning general councils representing the whole church. Here Huguccio took the lead. When Pope Gregory wrote that statutes of councils were established 'by universal consent' he was presumably not thinking of corporate consent in representative institutions. We might better translate his words by saying that the statutes were accepted 'by a general consensus' of the church. But Huguccio chose to gloss the phrase *universali consensu* with the words, 'Here is an argument on behalf of a corporation and that no one may withdraw from the canonical and common consent of his chapter or college or city as at *Dist.* 8 c.2.'[26] Similarly, Alanus wrote, 'Here is an argument that it is not permitted to a canon to dissent from his chapter.'[27] In these texts the general council was being treated as a corporate entity in a very technical sense. As for the representative nature of general councils, Huguccio and Alanus and Johannes Teutonicus all cited the Roman law maxim, *Quod omnes tangit ab omnibus approbetur* ('What touches all is to be approved by all'), as an argument that, when matters of faith were to be decided, even laymen should be represented at councils, since the preservation of the true faith was a matter that pertained to all Christians.[28]

Ideas like these were of central importance in fifteenth-century conciliar doctrines about the structure of the church, and by then they were being assimilated also into secular thought. In England a fourteenth-century common-law judge had already declared that 'parliament represents the body of the whole realm', and a later one added that 'The parliament of the king and the lords and the commons are a corporation.'[29] Later political thinkers would explain at length that a commonwealth, since it was conceived of as a single entity, not a mere collection of individuals, could be considered akin to a corporation, and that accordingly any assembly representing the single personality of the commonwealth must also be a corporate body. The early Decretists, who first expressed similar ideas in the realm of ecclesiology, offered no explanation for their views at all; instead they implied a whole structure of thought in half a dozen words, in a mere pattern of cross-references. We are in a world of *mentalités,* of taken-for-granted presuppositions rooted in the corporate life of the Middle Ages, that the canonists never explained because it never occurred to them that they needed any explanation.

It is the same when we turn to the theme of the secular commonwealth treated as a corporate entity. The idea that Christendom was made up of an assembly of states that recognized no temporal superior - the central

[26] *Summa ad Dist.* 15 c.2 (*Foundations*, p. 48).
[27] Gloss *ad Dist.* 15 c.2 ('Pope and Council', p. 213).
[28] All commenting on *Dist.* 96 c.4 (*Foundations*, p. 49).
[29] For these texts, and for a general discussion of the 'mystical body' of the state as a corporate entity see E. H. Kantorowicz, *The King's Two Bodies* (Princeton, 1957), pp. 207-32, esp. p. 225, 228.

concept of Grotius's seventeenth-century international law - was not invented by Grotius himself of course, nor by the fifteenth-century civic humanists, nor by Bartolus and his followers in the fourteenth century. It goes back to the works of our early Decretists. They came from many countries of Europe - England and France and Hungary and Spain as well as Germany and Italy. Some of them indeed saw the pope as a temporal overlord of all Europe, and some asserted that role for the emperor; but there were others who were disinclined to allow either claim. Ricardus Anglicus, writing in the 1190s, expressed this view most clearly. He first defended the view that each power, the spiritual and the temporal, was established by God and that neither was derived from the other. Then he turned to the theory of universal empire. Ricardus objected to it strenuously:

It is clear that many kings are not subject to the emperor . . . For we read of kings 'unconquered by command of the Lord' [Ecclesiastes 18.1], which we do not read of the emperor. Also the corporate body of a city can confer jurisdiction and imperium as at Novella 15 c.1. How much more that of a kingdom! . . . Again, when emperor and kings are annointed with the same authority, the same consecration, the same chrism, why should there be any difference between them as at C.16 q.1 c.5 [of the *Decretum*].[30]

It is an interesting text. Ricardus attributes to the national king an autonomous power derived from neither pope nor emperor but from the corporate body of the realm - the *universitas*. He supports this view by a deft interweaving of Roman law, canon law, and Scripture. Already before 1200, he is attributing to his king *iurisdictio et imperium*; and to a twelfth-century jurist the words implied a power to judge, to legislate, to command - all that would later be conveyed in the word 'sovereignty'. We are at the beginning of a theory of the national state.

During the thirteenth century, texts of this sort multiplied and they came from various countries - Spain and Sicily and France as well as England.[31] Joseph Strayer, after many years devoted to the study of French royal administration in the thirteenth century, recently concluded that the reality of a state certainly existed by then, but that perhaps there was no corresponding theory. Approaching the same topic through a study of medieval Roman and canon law, I had long been convinced that a theory of the state existed, but could never feel certain that there was any corresponding reality; it was pleasant to be reassured.

So far we have been considering the application of corporation theory to large-scale societies, what I called the macroscopic level of research. To investigate in detail canonistic ideas on the internal structure of corporations would take us to a rather microscopic level of inquiry. But the subject is too important to ignore altogether. In this sphere the canonists developed rules of private law that were soon transmuted into principles

[30] Gloss *ad Comp. I*, 4.18.17 in F. Gillmann, 'Richardus Anglicus als Glossator der Compilatio I', *Archiv für katholisches Kirchenrecht*, 107 (1927), 575-655 (p. 626).
[31] S. Mochi Onory, *Fonti canonistiche dell' idea moderna dello stato* (Milan, 1951), F. Calasso, *I Glossatori e la teoria della sovranità*, 3rd edn (Milan, 1957).

of constitutional law. They shaped in their discussions a whole new vocabulary - a vocabulary of ideas as well as of words - which became commonplaces of later political discourse. Constitutional thought here moved in a kind of spiral. In classical law the idea of the state preceded that of the corporation. The corporation was said to exist 'on the model of the state' (*ad exemplum reipublicae*).[32] Medieval canonists at several points modified and adapted the Roman law of corporations that they had inherited; then their new doctrines were used in turn to help define the institutions of the medieval state.

Canonistic analysis turned on technical phrases such as *maior et sanior pars* and *plena potestas* and *quod omnes tangit*. [33] All of these would be important in the evolution of later theories of representation and consent.

The *maior et sanior pars* was the 'greater and sounder part', which in canonistic doctrine could express the will of a corporate group. The canonists were not content with the simple numerical majority that sufficed in Roman law. In church assemblies they looked ideally for unanimity; the fact that dissension arose at all was a result of original sin, wrote Johannes Teutonicus. In any case, the really important consideration was that the right decision be adopted - the one supported by greater 'reason' or 'piety' or 'zeal' - and this might not always be the one favored by the greater number. This canonistic approach led to complications in actually conducting the affairs of corporate groups; it encouraged frequent appeals to higher authority against majority decisions. But the doctrine was important for political theory. Later thinkers used the term *sanior pars* (or similar expressions) when they wanted to attribute authority to a whole political community without handing over the actual conduct of affairs to the lowest classes who formed a numerical majority. Perhaps the best-known usage of this sort is the *valentior pars* ('weightier part') of Marsilius of Padua.

Plena potestas or *plena auctoritas* ('full power', 'full authority') were terms used to express the canonists' doctrine of representation. The words were borrowed from Roman law, but they acquired a new significance in canonistic writings because classical law had lacked an adequate doctrine of agency. In Roman law an individual or group could appoint an agent to negotiate with a third party, but the result of the transaction was to establish an obligation between the third party and the agent, not directly between the third party and the principal. In canon law, when a corporate group established a representative with 'full power', the group was directly obliged by the representative's acts, even when it had not consented to them in advance. Perhaps the canonists were encouraged to cut through the formalism of Roman law and adopt a more straightfor-

---

[32] *Dig.* 3.4.1.2.

[33] These legal phrases, and their various applications in medieval government, are discussed in more detail, with extensive modern literature, in Gaines Post, *Studies in Medieval Legal Thought* (Princeton, 1964).

ward theory of representation by their familiarity with the ancient theological concept of personification crystallized in Cyprian's phrase, 'the church is in the bishop'. Also the actual structure of medieval society encouraged such a development. Much of a canonist's day-to-day work dealt with the legal affairs of corporate ecclesiastical bodies that could act only through fully empowered agents.

The canonistic idea of representation 'with full power', first formulated as a principle of private law to define the role of a proctor acting for a corporation in a legal suit, acquired a constitutional significance when it was used to define the powers of members elected to representative assemblies. Many historians, especially English ones, have suggested that representative practices grew up gradually and naturally in medieval society without any conscious reflection on the principle involved. Up to a point this is true. In England, as early as 1086, spokesmen for each rural community gave information to the compilers of 'Domesday Book'; often chosen knights 'bore the record' of the shire to the king's central courts; in 1213 King John summoned knights from each shire 'to discuss the affairs of the realm'. Such practices were common in other countries too. But, when all is said, there is a gap between sending a messenger to report on local affairs or even to advise a king, and empowering a representative to bind a community by his decisions. The canonistic doctrine of *plena potestas* bridged the gap.

The formula was first used in connection with a political assembly in 1200 when Pope Innocent III summoned representatives with full power from a group of cities in the Papal States. In 1228 the elected representatives to the General Chapter of the Dominican Order had mandates of *plena potestas*. In 1231 Frederick II summoned representatives of Tuscan cities to attend an assembly with 'full authority'. By 1300 his example had been imitated in many parts of Europe. The term 'full power' first appeared in an English writ of summons to Parliament in 1268 and it appeared invariably from 1294 to 1872.

The third of our Roman law texts, *Quod omnes tangit ab omnibus approbetur* ('What touches all is to be approved by all'), was adapted by the canonists to express a generalized doctrine of consent. *Quod omnes tangit* is a genuine phrase of classical Roman law but in its original context in the Code it had no constitutional significance and was not even applied to corporations; it was a mere technicality of the private law of co-tutorship.[34] The canonists first applied the doctrine to corporate bodies, explaining that here the approval of the corporation as a whole was required, not that of each single member. Then they found new applications for it. There is perhaps a hint of this in a phrase of Rufinus (*c.* 1160): 'in a case which *touches* the whole church the pope can be judged by the church'.[35] A few years later another canonist restated the argument, this

[34] *Cod.* 5.59.5.
[35] *Summa ad Dist.* 21 c.4, ed. H. Singer, p. 46.

time with explicit reference to the text of the Code. Dealing again with a case of an erring pope, he wrote: 'just as what touches all is to be approved by all if it is good, so it should be rejected by all if it is evil as can be gathered from what is said in the Code at 5. 59. 5'.[36] Then around 1200, as we have seen, several Decretists used the phrase *quod omnes tangit* to explain the nature of general councils. At this point a decisive shift in meaning was occurring. A matter that 'touched' a whole community could be approved by a representative assembly acting on behalf of all.

Moving from theory to real life, in 1214 Pope Innocent III actually convoked a general council and to it summoned not only bishops but chosen representatives of cathedral chapters and collegiate churches because, he wrote, matters that concerned them were to be discussed. In 1225 a French church council appealed to the Roman law doctrine in a new way. A papal legate was seeking to exact contributions from the individual churches of France; the bishops complained that his demand should have been brought before the whole council since the issue was one that 'touched' all of them. Frederick II cited the whole phrase, *quod omnes tangit ab omnibus approbetur*, in summoning an imperial council in 1244. John of Viterbo, a Roman lawyer, borrowed the text back from the canonists and applied it to the government of Italian communes in 1261. The maxim was accepted as a normative principle of constitutional law in other countries during the second half of the thirteenth century. Edward I first incorporated *quod omnes tangit* into an English election writ in 1295 and by doing so, according to Stubbs, converted it 'from a mere legal maxim to a great and constitutional principle'.

The history of phrases like *plena potestas* and *quod omnes tangit* provides a good example of the interplay between secular and ecclesiastical ideas on government that characterized medieval thought and practice. The typical process that occurred was the assimilation of a text of Roman private law into church law, its adaptation and transmutation there to a principle of constitutional law, and then its reabsorption into the sphere of secular government in this new form. In this whole process, we need not suppose that any secular king deliberately decided to imitate in the government of his realm the practices of the church or of a particular group within the church, like a religious order. (Some scholars have suggested that the intricate representative system of the Dominican Order might have provided a model for secular government; others have found the idea highly improbable.) The truth is rather that similarities arose because the various parties involved - royal administrators, curial bureaucrats, organizers of new orders - were all drawing on a common pool of legal doctrines that they found both persuasive and useful. It is hard to see how medieval ideas and institutions could have assumed their characteristic forms had such material not been available.

---

[36] *Summa Reverentia sacrorum canonum ad Dist.* 40 c.6 ('Pope and Council', p. 216).

VARIETIES OF CORPORATION STRUCTURE

Much recent work has been devoted to the technicalities of medieval corporation theories.[37] But the underlying perception that the structure of a *universitas* could provide a model for the structure of the state is an old one. The point was made long ago by Gierke and Maitland; it is part of the conventional wisdom of all who deal with these matters. There remains, however, one final point where we must go a little beyond conventional wisdom.

Granted that the *universitas* became a model for the state (and the universal church), the constitutional theory that emerges depends greatly on the kind of *universitas* that is taken as a model. And, while there were hundreds of individual variations, medieval *universitates* fell into two major groups, which I shall call, with some slight oversimplification, the Roman law model and the canon law model.[38]

In the Roman law model of a corporation all power resided in the community and was delegated to an official who acted on behalf of the community. Similarly, in Roman constitutional law, the emperor derived his power from a grant by the people. This doctrine could have an absolutist form if the powers delegated were conceived of as permanently alienated, and indeed this was the most common teaching about imperial power among medieval Roman lawyers. But another point of view was possible. In the normal doctrine of Roman private corporation law, the agent's powers were not only derivative, but revocable and subject to modification. He represented the community as its delegate, its syndic. When this model was applied directly to large-scale political society it yielded a pure republicanism in which the chief magistrate could always be deposed by the will of the people. It also yielded a problem. How could a ruler be at once the people's sovereign and their subordinate agent? At the beginning of the thirteenth century, the Roman lawyer Azo found a solution in a distinction between the people as a corporate whole, a *universitas,* and the people as a collection of individuals.[39] The emperor was held to be greater than each individual so that each was subordinate to him; but he was not greater than the corporate whole from which his own power was derived. This argument was used later on by political thinkers as diverse as Mariana, a Jesuit, Hooker, an Anglican, and Buchanan, a Calvinist. In this theory the ruler held a position analogous to that of any elected official of a Roman law corporation.

The canon law model of a corporation was a more complex affair. It was based principally on the relations between a bishop and his cathedral chapter of canons. Here the chapter acted as an electoral body but it did not simply delegate its own authority to a chosen agent. Once elected

---

[37]   The best general survey is P. Michaud-Quantin, *Universitas. Expressions du mouvement communautaire dans le moyen-âge latin* (Paris, 1970).

[38]   Actually both types can be found in canon law but the second, 'complex' model is much more characteristic of church institutions.

[39]   For further discussion of this doctrine see pp. 58, 68, 74.

and consecrated, the bishop entered upon an office with its own inherent dignity, rights, and powers, derived not from the cathedral chapter but from the ancient constitution of the church, and so ultimately from God. A bishop was often called the 'head' of a corporate body to which the cathedral canons belonged as 'members'. This doctrine too could be given an absolutist form if the representation by the bishop was considered all-absorptive. Such a position was classically stated by Pope Innocent IV about 1250: 'Rectors assumed by corporations have jurisdiction and not the corporations themselves.' But the more common view was stated by the great jurist Hostiensis a few years later: 'What Innocent rejects is more true, although more difficult.'[40]

In the commonly accepted view, authority was shared between bishop and chapter; the bishop had his lands and rights, the canons theirs. (This was, incidentally, an actual fact of medieval life, essentially a feudal arrangement, to which church law had to accommodate itself.) The bishop, in a sense, represented or personified the whole church as its head, but the canons could and normally did appoint an agent, a proctor, who could specifically represent the chapter when their interests were involved. Thus canonistic corporation law found room for two types of representation, both of which would be significant for later constitutional thought: representation as a personification of the community in its head, and representation as a delegation of authority by a community to an agent. For the full representation of a cathedral church in a synod both types were necessary - both the bishop and a proctor of the chapter were summoned.

In case of episcopal vacancy or incapacity or gross negligence the bishop's jurisdiction might temporarily devolve to the chapter, and some later constitutional thinkers, applying this kind of corporation doctrine to general problems of government, made much of the possibility. But typically bishop and chapter ruled the church together. A major act involving the welfare of the whole church required the assent of both parties, the bishop and a majority of the canons. In this type of corporation one could not say that the bishop was less than the corporate body of the canons; he was at least co-equal with them. The canonists referred to a bishop as the 'principal part' or 'principal member' of his church. His assent was necessary for any major act of the corporation as a whole (as was the assent of the chapter). Applied to large-scale government this model of a corporation could yield, not a simple republicanism, but a complex doctrine of mixed or limited monarchy.

The details of medieval corporation law can grow wearisome. But the very language of constitutional discourse in the fifteenth century and still in the seventeenth century is hardly intelligible unless we have some acquaintance with the subject. At the Council of Constance in 1416 one

---

[40] Both authors were commenting on X.1.2.8.

spokesman argued that, although the pope was superior to each individual prelate, he was subordinate to the church as a whole. A pro-papal speaker replied that this was not so, since the pope was the 'principal member' of the church. In the debates over the powers of Parliament at the outbreak of the English Civil War, Henry Parker wrote that the king was greater than each individual, but less than the whole collected body of Parliament. John Bramhall, Bishop of Derry, replied that this was untrue, 'unless in that body you include His Majesty as principal member'.[41] Parker was arguing from Azo's Roman law doctrine of a corporation; Bramhall was arguing from Hostiensis's canon law doctrine of a corporation. Of course neither of them knew that that was what he was doing. Let us consider another example. Henry Parker also quoted the doctrine *Quod omnes tangit* ('What touches all is to be approved by all') from Edward I's election writ of 1295. Even if the authority of this text went back only to King Edward, Parker wrote, it would still be worthy of respect; but he thought that such a notable law was probably far more ancient and already existed in England before the Norman Conquest. We are back again to notions of primeval Teutonic freedom. Parker had no idea that the doctrine of *Quod omnes tangit,* as he used it, does indeed have a history that goes back beyond 1295, but that its earlier development is to be found in the canonistic glosses on Gratian's *Decretum.* Sometimes the writers at the end of the tradition that we are exploring did not themselves know the sources of the doctrines that they took for granted, that had become a part of the everyday furniture of their minds. For them the beginnings could easily be lost in the haze of a half-legendary past. From our standpoint we can see that such doctrines often had a quite specific origin in the juristic writings of the twelfth and thirteenth centuries.

[41]   Henry Parker, *Jus Populi* (London, 1644), p. 26. John Bramhall, *The Serpent-Salve* in *Works of John Bramhall,* III (Oxford, 1844), 325.

III

Origins of jurisdiction: hierarchy and consent, 1250-1350

So far we have considered some constitutional concepts of the medieval jurists. Between 1250 and 1350 their ideas were assimilated into new writings - a great body of them - which now dealt overtly with political philosophy. Often these writings were oddly preoccupied with problems concerning the origins of government; sometimes their authors suggested that the origin of all legitimate government must lie in the consent of the governed. These are the themes we shall explore next. They involve issues that remained of central importance in Western political thought down to the time of Grotius and Hobbes and Locke.

The new writing was stimulated partly by the rediscovery of Aristotle's *Politics,* partly by the real-life circumstances of the thirteenth century. The *Politics,* one of the last of Aristotle's works to be translated, opened up a new world of thought to medieval men. It showed them that political theory need not be merely a branch of jurisprudence; it could be an autonomous science in its own right, a proper field of study for philosophers. But, while the form of the new writing was influenced by Aristotle, its content was derived in large part from the actual experience of medieval society and from the reflections of earlier generations of jurists on that experience.

The content of the new political theory was also influenced by actual conflicts that occurred in the second half of the thirteenth century. New frictions arose between the secular and ecclesiastical hierarchies and within the ecclesiastical hierarchy itself. Toward 1300 a bitter clash between Pope Boniface VIII and King Philip the Fair of France raised fresh problems of church and state; from 1250 onward a simmering dispute between the papacy and the University of Paris stimulated new discussions on the right relationship between popes and bishops. Similar issues were involved in both controversies. The most extreme papal theorists held that all earthly jurisdiction inhered in the pope as vicar of God, and that kings and bishops alike were merely his servants and delegates. Since most kings and many bishops found these ideas unpalatable a great polemical literature of argument and counter-argument grew up. Major philosophers and theologians, familiar with the new Aristotelian learning and eager to deploy it, were drawn into the debates; but the problems they were debating were problems of their own world, often ones that Aristotle could never have dreamed of.

The application of Aristotelian forms of argument to medieval subject matter produced a new kind of political theorizing. Between 1250 and 1350 - from Thomas Aquinas to William of Ockham - a paradigmatic structure of ideas emerged, a framework of thought that defined the boundaries within which political discourse would be carried on for the next several centuries. This is especially true as regards our present topics - the origins of jurisdiction and consent as the basis of legitimacy.

THE MEANING OF JURISDICTION

Before we turn to these matters, there is a preliminary point that needs explaining - the sense in which I am using the term 'jurisdiction' (*jurisdictio*).[1] Nowadays the word is used mostly to describe the authority of a judge. But in seventeenth-century political thought 'jurisdiction' commonly meant the power of ruling in general, and 'supreme jurisdiction' was used as a synonym for *maiestas* or, in our modern word, 'sovereignty'. Historians have sometimes doubted whether such concepts existed in the Middle Ages at all; and certainly they were not much in evidence in the earlier medieval period. In early feudal society actual powers of government were widely diffused. Moreover the right to govern was confused then with all kinds of other rights and powers: with property rights in the secular world, with sacramental power of orders in the church and, in both spheres, with a mere capacity of the wise to discern pre-existing law so that, we are often told, 'law was found not made', 'a matter of knowledge rather than of will'. Again, in a feudal society rulership was based on an individual's personal loyalty to a lord, not on a community's obligation to a public ruling office. And because of all this, it is sometimes argued, the pure concept of sovereignty could not emerge until a later epoch when it was invented by Machiavelli or Bodin or Hobbes or whoever happens to be in fashion at any given time.

But the real change, the real turning point, came with the revival of Roman and canon law in the twelfth century. The doctrine of sovereignty, 'supreme jurisdiction', was expounded most enthusiastically by extreme supporters of papal monarchy; but around 1200 any competent Roman or canon lawyer could discriminate between ruling and owning, between jurisdiction and holy orders, between making law and finding law, between legislating and judging, between allegiance to a person and allegiance to an office. For them 'jurisdiction' was one of a cluster of terms used to define the idea of rulership (others were 'power', 'authority', 'prelacy', 'imperium'). 'Jurisdiction' was important because it com-

[1]   The fullest collection of illustrative texts is provided by Pietro Costa, *Iurisdictio. Semantica del potere politico nella pubblicistica medievale (1100-1433)* (Milan, 1969). See also M. Van de Kerckhove, 'La notion de juridiction dans la doctrine des décrétistes et des premiers décrétalistes', *Etudes franciscaines*, 49 (1937), 420-55, and E. Cortese, *La norma*, 2 vols. (Milan, 1964).

bined the ideas of rightfulness (from its etymological basis in *ius*) and of coercive force (from its definition in Roman law).[2] The word always retained its original limited sense as meaning the judicial authority of a magistrate to settle legal cases but it also came to acquire the broader meaning of ruling power in general. Thus Roman lawyers sometimes used the word jurisdiction to designate the complex of supreme legislative, judicial, and administrative rights received by the emperor when the Roman people bestowed on him 'all its power'. As Pillius wrote, 'Some jurisdiction is complete (*plena*) as in the human Prince, since the Roman people conferred on him all its power and imperium.' Bulgarus had already explained that the power of the emperor was different from that of a property-holder, since he ruled the empire 'by reason of jurisdiction, not of ownership'.[3] The jurists also distinguished between the enduring office of the imperium and the changing persons of the emperors.

Similar developments occurred in the writings of the canonists in the years around 1200. Alexander III drew a clear distinction between the person of a prelate and his ecclesiastical office in the influential decretal, *Quoniam abbas* - persons changed but the office remained always the same. Consideration of the role of archdeacons led to a distinction between jurisdiction and holy orders. Also the difference between jurisdiction and property-right was particularly evident in church law. A prelate exercised jurisdiction over his church; he did not own its property. (He could not alienate the goods of his church or otherwise freely dispose of them as his own.) To go through all the canonists' texts would take a treatise in itself. But one especially important one deserves mention. In introducing *Distinctio* 20 of the *Decretum*, Gratian offered a crucial definition. To interpret Scripture, he wrote, only knowledge or wisdom (*scientia*) was needed. But to settle legal cases not only knowledge was required but also power (*non solum scientia sed etiam potestas*).[4] Gratian's distinction here was a differentiation between the authority of a teacher and the authority of a ruler, between knowledge and will, between a capacity to discern and a right to command. He was arguing that, however superior in wisdom a man might be, his decisions had no juridical force unless he had acquired public authority. The distinction would be of central importance in later political theory. Gratian's language about wisdom and power, transmitted by Thomas Aquinas as well

[2] Accursius, in the Ordinary Gloss to the Digest, defined the 'pure imperium' of the highest magistrates, who could inflict capital punishment, as *plenissima iurisdictio*. He distinguished lower grades of jurisdiction as *plenior* and *semiplena*, *Digestum vetus* (Venice, 1598), Gloss *ad* 1.16.7. Accursius also defined jurisdiction (repeating an earlier formulation) as 'a power publicly introduced with responsibility for pronouncing what is right [*ius*] and enacting what is just [*aequitas*]'. Gloss *ad Dig.* 2.1.1.
[3] Pillius, *Summa de ordine iudiciorum*, 2.13 (Costa, p. 132). Bulgarus's view was reported by Accursius in the Ordinary Gloss to *Deo auctore* (Justinian's letter introducing the *Digest*).
[4] *Dist.* 20 *ante* c.1. 'It is one thing to settle legal cases, another to expound the Scriptures diligently. In settling legal affairs not only knowledge is required but also power. Therefore when Christ was about to say to Peter "Whatsoever you shall bind on earth . . ." he first gave to him the keys of the kingdom of heaven.'

as by a succession of jurists, was still being used by Richard Hooker in the sixteenth century.

In his dictum at *Dist.* 20, Gratian maintained that the 'power' needed to rule in the church was promised to Peter and his successors with the words 'I will give you the keys of the kingdom of Heaven.' The Decretists built an elaborate structure of argument around this text, often using the term 'jurisdiction' to expain it.

In doing so they came to understand the word as it is used in modern canon law, simply as a 'power of ruling', conceptually separable from the personal authority that inhered in a teacher of outstanding wisdom and from the sacramental power of orders that inhered in all priests.

In the course of their discussions on *Dist.* 20 the canonists also came to use the word jurisdiction to describe the supreme 'power of the keys' that Gratian here attributed to the papacy. Thus Laurentius tersely asserted, 'I believe the key to be jurisdiction', and Huguccio wrote, 'In deciding cases the authority of the Roman pontiffs prevails for . . . not only knowledge but also power is needed . . . power, that is jurisdiction.' Another contemporary Decretist linked the power of prelates to decide cases with the power to make law, 'the higher their place in judging, the more eminent place their statutes hold'; [5] and a generation later Innocent IV defined the pope's universal monarchy with the words 'the pope has jurisdiction and power' over all *de iure*.[6] The word jurisdiction still remained a little elusive; it had various meanings; but one of them was closely akin to the later idea of sovereignty.

The real-life controversies of the late thirteenth century gave rise to technical problems that led various political philosophers and theologians to deploy in their works the definitions and distinctions which the jurists had elaborated earlier. During the dispute between Boniface VIII and Philip the Fair, Giles of Rome argued that all rights of property and all rights of government descended from the pope as their source. In making this argument he so thoroughly confused, in the one word 'dominion', the concepts of jurisdiction and property that subsequent thinkers who wanted to attack his theocratic conclusions had to discriminate carefully between the two concepts. John of Paris, for instance, did so very crisply: 'To have proprietary right and ownership over property is not the same as having jurisdiction over it', he wrote; 'Princes have the power of judging even though they do not have ownership of the property in question.'[7]

---

[5]   *Summa Antiquitate et tempore ad Dist.* 20 *ante* c.1 ('Pope and Council', p. 201 n. 22). For the comment of Huguccio see *Foundations*, p. 32 n. 1, and, for Laurentius, Van de Kerckhove, p. 441 (where the text is mistakenly attributed to Johannes Teutonicus). See also *Origins*, pp. 41-5, for further comments on Gratian's text.

[6]   *In quinque libros decretalium commentaria* (Venice, 1570), *Com. ad* X.3.34.8 [X = *Liber extra*, i.e. *Decretales Gregorii IX*].

[7]   *De potestate regia et papali*, ed. F. Bleienstein, *Johannes Quidort von Paris. Über königliche und päpstliche Gewalt* (Stuttgart, 1969). Quotations in the text above generally follow the

At about the same time, a quite fortuitous stimulus to discussions on jurisdiction - again drawing the concept from the technical works of the jurists into the arena of general debate - came from the abdication of Pope Celestine V in 1294. Critics of the abdication argued that, since papal power was bestowed by God alone, it could be taken away only by God. Just as a priest, once ordained, could not cease to be a priest, so too, they argued, the supreme priest could not cease to be supreme priest. Defenders of the abdication, and eventually everyone came to accept it as a valid act, had to distinguish in the first place between jurisdiction and sacramental orders. (The distinguishing quality that made the pope 'supreme priest' was precisely a supremacy of jurisdiction; he could relinquish that power without relinquishing the power of orders.) In the second place, to counter the argument that only God could take away papal jurisdiction they had to distinguish between jurisdiction as it inhered in the office of the papacy and in the person of the pope. We can again conveniently illustrate both distinctions from the work of John of Paris: 'The power of orders is indelible', he wrote; 'But jurisdiction is another matter: just as it can be increased or diminished so it can be deleted and taken away.' On the distinction between person and office, John wrote: 'Although the papacy in itself is from God alone, yet in so far as it is in this or that person, it comes through human cooperation . . . it can, then, by human agreement cease to exist in this or that man.' Every author who wrote to defend Celestine's abdication (even so zealous a papalist as Giles of Rome) had to make these points. Peter Olivi, in his discussion of the case, wrote expressively that all jurisdiction as it inhered in a person, even a pope, was *mobilis* - movable or removable - and the perception remained important for the future.[8] A seventeenth-century author wrote of sovereignty: 'It's easily separable from man and man from it.'

By 1300 then a concept of jurisdiction as the characteristic power inhering in a ruling office was emerging in both law and political theory. We can now turn back to the issues raised at the outset. Our problem is to explain why so much subsequent political thought became focussed on the question of the origin of jurisdiction and how a generalized theory of consent arose. It may be helpful in addressing these questions to define a little more closely the idea of 'government by consent'. The main features of the doctrine, as it was classically formulated in the seventeenth and eighteenth centuries, have been summed up thus: 'Political obligations are derivative from the consent of those who create a government (sometimes a society) . . . legitimacy and duty depend on consent, on a voluntary individual act, or rather on a concatenation of voluntary individual acts, and not on patriarchy, theocracy, divine right, the natural

translation by J. A. Watt, *John of Paris. On Royal and Papal Power* (Toronto, 1971). On property and jurisdiction see Bleienstein, p. 98; Watt, p. 106.

[8]   John of Paris, Bleienstein, pp. 208, 202; Watt, pp. 251, 244. Peter Olivi, *De renuntiatione*, ed. L. Oliger, in *Archivum Franciscanum Historicum*, 11 (1918), 309-73 (p. 356).

superiority of one's "betters", the "naturalness" of political life, necessity, custom, convenience, psychological compulsion, or any other basis.'⁹ One might add that, although the 'naturalness' or 'necessity' of political life do not in themselves imply a theory of consent, the doctrine was commonly defended in early modern thought by appeals both to natural law and to utility.

It has been pointed out often enough that the 'voluntarism' of consent theory owes something to a religious tradition that emphasized the will as much as the intellect. We can perhaps go a little further and relate the origins of the doctrine more specifically to problems of medieval ecclesiology and medieval society. After attempting to do this in rather general terms, I want to consider the distinctive contributions of four specific fourteenth-century thinkers - Hervaeus Natalis, Durandus of St Pourçain,¹⁰ Marsilius of Padua, and William of Ockham. The first two were orthodox medieval Catholics (and Hervaeus in particular was a rather extreme defender of centralized papal power); the other two were condemned as heretics. Two of the authors (the heretics) figure prominently in any standard text-book on the history of political theory; the others are seldom mentioned. All of them combined religious and secular modes of thinking in ways that contributed significantly to the growth of Western consent theory.

ORIGINS OF JURISDICTION

Let us begin with the question of origins. Among the treatises written in the late thirteenth and early fourteenth centuries one encounters titles such as *On the Origin of Jurisdiction*, *On the Cause of Ecclesiastical Power*, *On the Birth of Empire*. The problem they addressed was bequeathed to political theory by the canonists, and especially by Pope Innocent IV, a hard and unscrupulous man but a great lawyer. At one point in his commentary on the *Decretales* (*c.* 1250) he raised his eyes from the dusty technicalities of canon law to glance over the whole history of human government. Addressing specifically the problem whether licit government could exist among infidels, he wrote:

By nature all men are free . . . I read of just and rightful jurisdiction where the sword given for vengeance is mentioned . . . But how this jurisdiction first began I do not know unless perhaps God assigned some person to do justice . . . or unless in the beginning the father of a family had complete jurisdiction over his family by the law of nature though now he has it only in a few minor matters . . . Or again, a people could have princes by election as they had Saul and many others . . . I maintain therefore that lordship, possession and jurisdiction can belong to infidels licitly . . . for these things were made not only for the faithful but every

⁹ P. Riley, 'How Coherent is the Social Contract Tradition?', *Journal of the History of Ideas*, 34 (1973), 543-62.
¹⁰ Or pseudo-Durandus. The authorship of the relevant work is disputed. See n. 37.

rational creature . . . For God makes his sun to shine on the wicked, and he feeds the birds of the air.[11]

It is a very good passage for such a very bad pope. Also it had a great future. Innocent's doctrine was repeated in the fifteenth-century debates about the activities of the Teutonic Knights in pagan Lithuania, and it was transmitted by late medieval jurists to Spanish authors of the sixteenth century. They applied it in a quite novel context, to defend the rights of American Indians. The Indies debates in turn influenced the work of Grotius and the subsequent growth of seventeenth-century doctrines on international law. If we were pursuing that particular theme Innocent's text would seem of major importance in the evolution of thought from the medieval canonists to the early modern world. For our present purpose we may note that Innocent posed very clearly the problem of origins and hit neatly on the three possible sources of legitimacy that would be discussed for centuries - patriarchal authority, direct divine right, or government by election and consent.

Of course the problem of origins goes back further. Classical authors too had sometimes discussed the beginnings of government. Aristotle described a natural evolution from the family to the clan to the perfect society of the polis. Cicero offered an alternative Stoic version, a less naturalistic, more conventional account of the origin of the state, based on a coming together of people who had formerly lived solitary lives. Both accounts were well known in the Middle Ages. John of Paris began his treatise *On Royal and Papal Power* with Aristotle's version and followed it immediately with Cicero's. He seems to have regarded the two as complementary to one another. 'Since man is by nature created a political and civil animal, as is said in Book I of the *Politics* . . . he must of necessity live in a community', John wrote. Then he added: 'Since these men could not . . . bring themselves to live the common life natural to them . . . others . . . tried to bring them by more persuasive arguments to an ordered life in common under one ruler, as Cicero says.'[12] The co-existence of these two points of view has sometimes been regarded as a characteristic of sixteenth-century political theory;[13] but the combination of Aristotelian naturalism with Stoic conventionalism was common enough from around 1300 onward.

To return to our problem. The major point is that, in classical works, accounts of the origin of the state are not of central importance in the whole structure of political thought. For Aristotle or Cicero they are just a kind of throat clearing before the author gets down to the serious busi-

---

[11] *Com. ad* X. 3.34.8.

[12] Bleienstein, pp. 75, 77; Watt, pp. 77, 79.

[13] See e.g. J. H. M. Salmon, *The French Religious Wars in English Political Thought* (Oxford, 1959). Quentin Skinner, *Foundations of Modern Political Thought,* 11, also emphasizes a revived Stoicism as an important element in early modern political theory. But the Stoicism was always there, at least after the renewal of Roman law studies in the twelfth century.

ness of analyzing how political man behaves or ought to behave, how constitutions work or ought to work. But from John of Paris to John Locke, and beyond to Rousseau, political theorists frequently began their works with hypotheses (sometimes very odd ones) about the origins of government, which determined the whole content of the argument that followed. So when we read the great classics of Western political theory – Rousseau, Locke, Hobbes, Grotius – over and over again we find ourselves drawn into a strange science-fiction world of imaginary individuals without societies, or imaginary societies without governments, a most unnatural state of nature, a parable, a paradox, at the foundation of serious political thinking.

One reason for all this, I think, is well understood in relation to works of the seventeenth and eighteenth centuries. When theorists purported to investigate the origins of political authority they were really trying to explain the grounds of political legitimacy. But this form of argument has a medieval background. From the thirteenth century onward men were asking Rousseau's questions. Man is born free. Everywhere we see him bound. How did it come about? What can make it legitimate? Medieval men did not say literally, 'Everywhere he is in chains', but they often used the word *ligare* – men were bound by laws, bound by government. And sometimes, as we shall see with Hervaeus Natalis, they wrote *obligare* and asked how men could come to be obliged. They were addressing the question that has been with us ever since, the question of political obligation.

When all this is understood we are still left with an unresolved problem. Why did the first association of individuals into political groups seem so important? Or, to put it differently: How did the tradition begin of addressing the real problem of obligation through the pseudo-problem of origins? There are several complementary answers and they involve the same kinds of issue that we encountered in approaching the thought of the twelfth-century jurists – patterns of society, specific conflicts involving the church, revivals of ancient thought in a medieval context.

In the first place, the corporative structures of medieval society are again significant. We are dealing with a time when, all over Europe, separated individuals were in real life coming together, swearing oaths to one another, covenanting together to form new societies, sometimes political societies – all those *universitates,* guilds, colleges, communes that we noticed earlier – and were deliberately shaping constitutional structures for their new societies. For civil and canon lawyers one distinction between a *universitas* and a mere crowd of individuals consisted precisely in the fact that the *universitas,* but not the individuals, could create a ruling official, having ordinary jurisdiction over the community. This doctrine of the lawyers paralleled and perhaps helped to prepare the way for the teaching of some later political theorists that a 'contract of society' had to precede a 'contract of government'. For the jurists a *universitas* had to be formed before jurisdiction could be conferred.[14] We are sometimes misled by the medieval word *consuetudo,* 'custom', into supposing that such developments took place slowly and imperceptibly, that medieval men themselves were hardly aware of what was going on. But when medieval people 'chose' customs they were often engaged in what we should call legislation, sometimes constitutional legislation. As early as 1127 the burghers of St Omer were granted a right 'to correct their customary laws from day to day'.[15] During the thirteenth century such grants could deploy all the sophisticated language of Roman and canon law. In 1230 the little town of Ile-Jourdain received a charter granting to the community (*universitas*) the right to elect a representative council (*capitulum*) to which all should swear an oath. The council had 'full and free power' (*plena et libera potestas*) to abolish or change burdensome customs, written and unwritten, and to make and institute new ones.[16] This was a very deliberate shaping of the legal structure of a society; and such activity was taking place in innumerable thirteenth-century communities. When the establishment of a new commune was involved, we are dealing precisely with 'a concatenation of voluntary, individual acts', operating to 'create a government', to constitute a political community where none had existed before.

In the sphere of ecclesiastical life we find similar examples. The notion that 'the individual' was invented by religious or humanist reformers of the sixteenth century is happily outmoded; so too are vague murmurings about 'group-personality' in the Middle Ages. On the other hand, much recent writing has emphasized the new personalism or humanism evident in twelfth-century spirituality. One such work, an interesting and perceptive one by Colin Morris, was called *The Discovery of the Individual, 1060-1200.* But the religious life of the age - like the religious life of the Reformation era - was characterized as much by corporatism as by individualism; that is to say new forms of community life were as much in evidence as new forms of personal devotion. The leaders of the Cistercian Order pioneered in both spheres and, *mutatis mutandis,* one might say the same of Calvin or Ignatius Loyola. Moreover, in the twelfth century, the 'corporatism' and the 'individualism' were not really contradictory. (Medieval canon law even found room for carefully specified individual rights within corporate structures.) Perhaps it is only when persons become more sharply aware of themselves as individuals that they need to reflect consciously on the rules by which they form themselves into ordered groups.

For us, in any case, the essential point is that during the twelfth and

14 E.g. Accursius, Ordinary Gloss *ad Cod.* 3.13.3; Innocent IV, *Com. ad* X.1.31.3. For the parallel doctrine in later political thought see pp. 73-4, 98.
15 H. Pirenne, *Medieval Cities* (Princeton, 1952), p. 192, citing Galbert of Bruges.
16 E. Cabie, *Chartes de coutumes inédites de la Gascogne Toulousaine* (Paris-Auch, 1884), p. 21.

thirteenth centuries many new communities - both religious and secular - were coming into existence through acts of voluntary consent on the part of the members who formed them, and that much deliberate reflection about the right ordering of such communities was taking place. It seems to me comprehensible that men living in a society with so much everyday experience of this sort might readily approach the problem of political obligation by considering the original constituting of political societies.

If, however, this approach seems too vaguely sociological, one can point to a more simple, practical reason why medieval political theorists had to write extensively about the origins of government. The necessity grew out of the conflict between church and state. A twelfth-century commentary on Gratian's *Decretum* began with the words, *Antequam essent clerici* ('Before there were any clerics, kings ruled in France'). The argument was taken up a century later by John of Paris and other publicists of Philip the Fair. 'Royal power existed in its own right both in principle and practice before papal power', John wrote, 'and there were kings before there were any Christians in France'.[17] John's opening paragraphs about the origin of government were essential to his whole subsequent argument because they explained how legitimate rulership could have arisen in the first place without any papal intervention. The assertion that kings existed before popes became a standard royalist argument; and the assertion that bishops were at least coeval with popes became a standard episcopalist argument. The implication was that neither royal nor episcopal power could have been derived from the pope in the first place. Such arguments were not necessarily conclusive. A papalist could reply that there always had existed an order of ruling priests, and a head of the order, prefigured in the Old Testament. Or he might argue that the whole political order of the world had been transformed with the coming of Jesus Christ. But he could not grapple with his opponents at all without responding to their arguments about how legitimate government first came to be constituted.

Once we have understood why questions of political theory were often approached in this particular way we can begin to see how the problem of obligation became interwoven with the problem of origins. Royalist and papalist writers had to establish not only priority in time but also intrinsic legitimacy for the systems of government they defended. And, in attempting to do this, they had to deal not only with the problems of their own age but also with a notable incoherence in the traditions they had inherited from the past. It was not only that, in the practical world of affairs, the claims of popes conflicted with those of kings. Equally intransigently, in the world of pure thought, the ideas of Augustine conflicted with those of Aristotle.

[17] Bleienstein, p. 113; Watt, p. 124.

Augustine held that God had intended men to be lords over irrational creatures, not over one another - 'not man over man, but man over beast', he wrote. For Augustine slavery and political subjection were both consequences of sin. States had arisen through the lust for power of strong men who imposed their wills on weaker neighbors. God permitted this for two reasons. The state of subjection into which most men fell was a fitting punishment for sin; and the discipline that even bad rulers imposed provided a partial remedy for sin in that it restrained men from indulging to the full the criminal proclivities of fallen nature.

This rather gloomy view of political authority prevailed all through the early Middle Ages. In the eleventh century Pope Gregory VII restated it with enthusiasm, almost gleefully, in his polemics against King Henry IV of Germany. Then men of the thirteenth century encountered a radically different vision of the state, its origins and purpose, in Aristotle's *Politics*. For Aristotle the state was natural to man. Political obligation was simply taken for granted because man could fulfill his moral potentialities, could become fully, truly human only in a political society. By definition civilized men lived in a *civitas*, a polis. They yielded to it their highest loyalty and they freely accepted the laws and sanctions it imposed. The end of the state was to promote the public good. The central problem of political theory was to determine what form of constitution could best serve that end over the longest period of time.

Thirteenth-century men found this new vision enticing, irresistible indeed. And yet they could not simply apply it unmodified to their own society. They could not give all their loyalty to the state; the church had its claims too, surpassing claims for most medieval people. And Aristotle had not answered adequately the question that Augustine had placed at the heart of Christian political thought. Let us grant that the state is natural to man. Still the question remains: Why should this man rule and that man serve, this man command and that man obey, this one punish and that one suffer? How did it all begin? What could make it legitimate?

CONSENT: PRACTICE AND THEORY

At first glance the answer may seem obvious. Consent can create government and endow it with legitimacy. But although this is a possible answer it is really by no means an obvious one. When Thomas Jefferson wrote in 1786 that all legitimate government was based on consent he did indeed seem to be uttering a platitude. The American founding fathers had found this teaching in many respected natural law theorists of the preceding century - Pufendorf, and Locke and even Hobbes in his way; hence the Declaration of Independence could assert with untroubled confidence that the doctrine of consent was 'self-evident'. Modern historians of American constitutional thought often begin by writing that we can of course take such Lockean generalities for granted and then move on to sophisticated discourse about specific American variations on the common theme. But, for a historian viewing the matter in broader perspective, the precise problem is to explain how the Lockean platitude about legitimacy and consent grew into existence in the first place; for, like many 'self-evident' truths, this one has not been evident at all to most of the human race over most of recorded history.

I am reminded of a distinguished literary scholar from Northern Ireland, C. S. Lewis. He wrote once of romantic love, also a medieval invention, and observed that to us it seems entirely natural to suppose that such love can be an 'ennobling passion', a central theme of life and literature. Then he added that we can at once see how unnatural our supposition is if we imagine ourselves trying to explain it to Aristotle or St Paul or Virgil or the author of *Beowulf*. We might apply the same test to our common supposition that all legitimate government is based on consent. Aristotle would tell us that government is legitimate when it seeks the common good; St Paul would say it is legitimate because the powers that be are ordained by God; Virgil might mention the maintenance of universal peace and order; I am not sure about the author of *Beowulf* but he would perhaps refer to prowess and right of blood. All of our authors could have found room for consent in their different worlds of thought, but they would have seen it as a consequence rather than a cause. When the power of government was perceived to serve the common good, to be ordained by God, to maintain peace, to be wielded by a great leader, men would readily assent to such government. But none of our authors would have written, as Marsilius of Padua wrote, that consent was the 'efficient cause' of licit government. It is a typical example of how medieval men used Aristotelian terminology - often imagining that they were simply paraphrasing Aristotle - but really reaching conclusions that could have grown only out of the religious culture and social life of their own times.

When we look at these realities of medieval life, the growth of a formal theory of government by consent may seem natural enough. Medieval society was indeed saturated with consensual practices. Feudal contracts were based on mutual consent. Innumerable corporate groups chose their leaders by consent. Kings summoned assemblies to consent to taxation. Church government was a structure of elective offices. Canon lawyers had inherited from Pope Leo I the principle that 'He who rules over all is to be chosen by all', and civil lawyers were taught that the Roman people created an emperor by conferring their own authority on him. In actual practice, in the thirteenth century, popes and emperors were chosen by election, and the elections were often bitterly contested affairs in which a hard-to-achieve 'concatenation of voluntary individual acts' was needed to achieve a successful outcome. Besides all this, medieval intellectuals knew Cicero's saying (handed down by Augustine) that a political community was a multitude associated 'by consent', and they were familiar with the Stoic doctrines that men were by nature equal and by nature free. Such principles, taken in association with medieval practices, could provide persuasive grounds for an argument that licit government could be based only on the consent of the governed.

The universally held belief that all power came ultimately from God might seem an obstacle to the development of such a doctrine. But here the canon and civil lawyers had already prepared the ground for the position - very commonly asserted in early modern constitutional theory - that power came from God through the people. Laurentius wrote (*c.* 1210): 'The people through election makes an emperor but not the empire [*imperium*], just as the cardinals promote someone to a jurisdiction that is given by God.' Huguccio also mentioned both a divine and a popular origin of imperial authority: 'Here it can clearly be gathered that each power, the apostolic and the imperial, was instituted by God and that neither is derived from the other - the emperor has the power of the sword and the imperial dignity from election by the princes and people.'[18] Similar ideas were often expressed by Roman lawyers too. Thus, Cynus of Pistoia explained, 'It is not absurd that imperium should be derived from God and the people. The emperor is from the people, but the imperium is called divine from God.'[19] An eminent theologian, Stephen Langton, offered a variation on this theme in discussing the origin of royal power. Langton suggested that the two 'swords' of spiritual and temporal power were both given to the church by God; but then he added at once, 'I say to the church, not to the pope.' Royal authority could indeed be said to derive from the church, he held, but only when the church was understood as the whole Christian people, the congregation of the faithful.[20]

From the thirteenth century onward, this line of argument was developed by political philosophers and theologians in two ways. In the first way, God was presented only as a remote first cause. Thus Peter Aureoli argued that God did not directly institute government among men; rather he endowed men with natural reason, and natural reason then perceived the need to institute government and to choose rulers. In this form of argument the existence of God is presumed, but he is not a necessary hypothesis; the discussion could just as well begin from empirical observation of man's rational nature.[21] Alternatively, one could per-

---

18 Laurentius, Gloss *ad Comp.* III, 1.5.1; Huguccio, *Summa ad Dist.* 96 c.6 (Mochi Onory, *Fonti canonistiche*, pp. 196, 148). The image of a ruler's 'sword' bestowed on him 'from God by the people' recurs in the sixteenth-century *Vindiciae contra tyrannos*; H. J. Laski (ed.), *A Defence of Liberty against Tyrants* (London, 1924), p. 120.
19 *Commentaria ad Dig.* 1.4.3. For this and related Roman law texts see Cortese, *La norma*, pp. 200-2, with the literature cited there.
20 Stephen's text was printed by J. W. Baldwin, *Masters, Princes and Merchants*, II (Princeton, 1970), 110-11.
21 Peter Aureoli, *Commentarium* (Rome, 1596), *In Sent* II d.44 art. 3, *In Sent* IV d.36. On these texts see G. de Lagarde, *La naissance de l'esprit laique au déclin du moyen âge*, II (Paris, 1958), 297-301. The same teaching is found in Durandus of St Pourçain, *De iurisdictione ecclesiastica* (Paris, 1506), fol. 1rb, and Hervaeus Natalis, *De potestate pape* (Paris, 1647), p. 366.

ceive God as more actively at work in guiding the choice of the community. John of Paris perhaps had this in mind when he referred to emperors created by the people 'through the inspiration of God'.[22] More explicitly Bonaventure, considering the choice of a pope, described election as 'the way of the Spirit', a process in which the Holy Spirit worked to produce a consensus of hearts and minds.[23] In the fifteenth century Nicholas Cusanus built a whole ecclesiology and political theory around this doctrine. I think it was often tacitly presumed in later thought - perhaps unconsciously - even when it was not explicitly stated.

Given the whole background of medieval thought and practice, it is not surprising that every major work on law and political theory written around 1300 contains at least some passing reference to consent. Among the canonists, Hostiensis argued from the particular right of the Roman people in the election of an emperor to a generalized doctrine of consent to government. The Roman people held their right, he wrote, 'by the common law according to which every corporate body elects a ruler for itself'. (The lesser *universitates* were again serving as models for political structures.) Then Hostiensis added: 'Or from natural reason on which law is based as in Institutes 1.2 and *Dist*. 1 c.5'. Here again a canonist was suggesting a whole theory of government in half a dozen words and a couple of cross-references.[24] Among the philosophers, perhaps Duns Scotus has the most interesting passage. He envisaged a multitude of unrelated strangers coming together to build a city. No natural patriarchal authority would exist among them, but they might come to need a government. In order to institute one, Duns wrote, they could all assemble together and submit themselves either to one person or to the whole community (thus giving us so to speak a choice between Hobbes and Locke at the start of the tradition).[25]

HIERARCHY: NATURE AND GOD

After all this can we not say that - even if it is not true of all civilizations in general - still it is true of our thirteenth-century civilization in particular that a doctrine of consent as the basis of all just government would indeed emerge naturally, inevitably, really self-evident to any reasonable man? Unfortunately there is still a difficulty. Medieval minds were fascinated, captivated by an alternative vision - the vision of hierarchy. In real life they were ruled by hierarchies of government in church and state. But beyond this they perceived the whole universe as a great hierarchical chain of being. From God authority flowed to an angelical hierarchy in heaven and to an ecclesiastical hierarchy on earth according to the neo-

[22] Bleienstein, p. 173; Watt, p. 203.
[23] *De perfectione evangelica*, 4.3 in *Opera omnia*, v (Quaracchi, 1891).
[24] *Comm. ad* X.1.6.33.
[25] *Opus Oxoniense*, 4.15.2 in *Opera omnia*, xviii (Paris, 1894).

Platonic doctrine of pseudo-Dionysius - and there was an enthusiastic revival of Dionysian studies at Paris in mid thirteenth century. In this world-view the legitimacy of a ruler did not depend on consent from below but on a position in a hierarchy of being ordained from above. The doctrine of hierarchy, usually associated with divine-right monarchy, persistently attracted able minds from the twelfth century to the seventeenth. It provided a simple response to a question that otherwise was not easy to answer within the framework of commonly accepted assumptions. How could some persons licitly exercise power over others unless God, the supreme governor of the whole universe, had established them as rulers among men? Moreover there seemed abundant evidence that the whole of nature was hierarchically ordered. Celestial bodies, so everyone believed, controlled the motion of lower ones; dominance hierarchies could be discerned in animals; among the social insects all the bees of a hive were seen to serve one ruler. (Mere patriarchal prejudice perhaps explains the fact that, down to the eighteenth century, the ruler of the hive was always referred to as a king rather than a queen.) To medieval men, divinely ordained hierarchy seemed, not just an abstract theory, but an observable fact of nature.

The doctrine of hierarchy found a classical formulation in Boniface VIII's bull, *Unam sanctam.*

> According to the blessed Dionysius . . . in the order of the universe . . . the lowest are ordered by intermediaries and inferiors by superiors . . . if the earthly power errs it shall be judged by the spiritual, if the lesser spiritual power errs it shall be judged by the greater spiritual power, but if the supreme spiritual power errs it can be judged by God alone.

But papal theocracy was not the only form of hierarchical doctrine in the thirteenth century. Royalist authors, instead of appealing to consent, could simply argue that God had established two hierarchies of government among men. William of Auvergne applied pseudo-Dionysian hierarchical ideas to the government of France. Such ideas permeate the political thought of Thomas Aquinas too, along with his well-known Aristotelianism.

Thomas is sometimes regarded as an originator of the doctrine of government by consent - and there were important populist elements in his work which we shall consider later - but when he discussed the origin of government and the grounds of its legitimacy the hierarchical elements in his thought were preponderant. He saw the state as a work of art. That is no invention of Renaissance humanism. But the whole point of the comparison for him and for many contemporaries was that art imitated nature and that nature displayed a natural order of subordination of the many to the one. In the *De regno* Thomas wrote, 'The members of the body are moved by one heart . . . among bees there is one king . . . and in the whole universe God is maker and ruler of all. So if art imitates nature and the work of art is better the closer the imitation, it follows that a multitude of men should be ruled by one [king].'[26] As for who that king should be, Thomas wrote in the *Summa contra Gentiles*, 'He who excels in intellect naturally rules.' To prove this Thomas cited both Aristotle's *Politics* and the Old Testament ('The fool shall serve the wise');[27] then he plunged again into a disquisition on the hierarchical ordering of the universe as a whole. Such texts provide an interesting mixture of Aristotle, Scripture, and neo-Platonism, but they have nothing to do with a doctrine of government by consent; and there are dozens of such passages in medieval political theory. My favorite is one from Engelbert of Admont where, in a single dense paragraph, the author managed to include everything from the celestial hierarchy of the heavens to the pecking order of chickens, not forgetting to mention the king of the bees along the way.[28]

It is tempting to dismiss such argumentation as mere gothic fantasy - beasts and bees and birds (chickens indeed) as a basis for serious political theory! But now scientists have again taken to studying the social insects and dominance hierarchies in birds and animals for insights into the natural bases of human behavior. Konrad Lorenz was awarded a Nobel Prize for such work. The argument from animal hierarchies to human hierarchies may be mere nonsense; probably it is nonsense; but it is not just medieval nonsense. The human mind has never ceased to be fascinated by natural hierarchy; and the point that hierarchical ordering is a near-universal manifestation among human cultures seems self-evident.

Hence, in spite of all the consensual practices of medieval society, it was still no easy task around 1300 to produce a coherent, generalized theory that all licit jurisdiction was based on the consent of the governed.

FOUR FOURTEENTH-CENTURY THEORISTS

The task called for a sophisticated analysis of the concept of jurisdiction itself, a distinction between the natural superiority of the wise man and the right to govern of a legitimate ruler, and an explanation of how the real-life governing hierarchies of church and state could be fitted into a framework of consent theory. All this was first achieved adequately by Hervaeus Natalis, a professor of theology at the University of Paris who became master-general of the Dominican Order, writing about 1315, just a few years before Marsilius of Padua. He was, as we noted earlier, a rather extreme papalist. His originality was to demonstrate that the papal claims could be defended by a very rigorously argued theory of consent if we granted only the premise that the papal office was originally founded by God, a premise that almost everyone did grant at that time. Hervaeus's views are set out in two short treatises, *De iurisdictione* and

---

[26] *De regno*, 1.2 in *Opera omnia*, XXVII (Paris, 1889).
[27] *Contra Gentiles*, 3.81 in *Opera*, XII.
[28] *De ortu et fine Romani imperii* in M. Goldast, *Politica imperialia* (Frankfurt, 1614), p. 754.

De potestate pape.[29] He began both works by asking, 'What is jurisdiction?' Philologically, he explained, the word meant simply *jus dicere*, 'to say the law' or 'say what is right'. But any wise man could say what was right and this did not confer jurisdiction on him, for legal jurisdiction included the authority to use coercive force. (The canonists' distinction between 'knowledge' and 'power' was implicit here.) Hervaeus distinguished therefore. He was not writing about any form of private jurisdiction such as a father had over a son. Nor was he concerned with the academic authority of a teacher judging of some matter in the schools. His subject, he declared in the *De iurisdictione*, was to be 'public or political jurisdiction - such as kings and princes have in temporal affairs or popes and prelates in spiritual affairs'.[30] Hervaeus next offered an explanation that was crucial to his whole argument. The distinctive characteristic of public jurisdiction was not simply that its holder said what was right; also his pronouncements had binding force; they created obligation. The community was obliged to accept as just what the holder of jurisdiction decreed; and this was indeed the precise difference between a ruler and a private individual. 'A prudent man without jurisdiction can provide guidance by means of advice or teaching. . . . He cannot oblige. . . . The power of judging that belongs to one having jurisdiction implies something further, that the community is obliged.'[31] The obligation of the people in turn justified the coercive sanctions that rulers imposed.

Hervaeus also analyzed the content of jurisdiction. It consisted, he wrote in the *De potestate*, of two powers, which were exercised in legislating and in judging (*statuendo vel sententiando*). In the *De iurisdictione* he added a third power, the power to execute the laws.[32] It is, so far as I have noticed, the first formal description of the powers of government as legislative, judicial, and executive. But, just as when the tripartite division was revived in the seventeenth century, the executive power was considered inferior, by no means coequal with the other two. We are still a long way from Montesquieu.

But we are not so very far from Locke. For Hervaeus next asked: How is jurisdiction acquired? And he answered: 'Only by consent of the people' (*per solum consensum populi*). Jurisdiction did not inhere in any person by nature, for by nature all men were equal. If anyone held jurisdiction without consent he held it by violence, and violence conferred no right. It was indeed fitting that a wiser and better man should rule, but these qualities did not in themselves confer jurisdiction. If such a man tried to

---

[29] *De iurisdictione*, ed. L. Hödl (Munich, 1959); *De potestate pape* (Paris, 1647).
[30] *De iur.*, p. 14.
[31] *De iur.*, p. 15. *De pot.*, pp. 363-4. The distinction became classical in later political theory. Pufendorf wrote, 'Law differs from *Counsel* in this, that by the latter a Man . . . has no proper power so as that he can lay any direct obligation . . .' (*Law of Nature*, 1.6.1). Pufendorf's words were quoted by James Wilson, the federalist author mentioned on pp. 55, 78.
[32] *De pot.*, p. 364. *De iur.*, p. 15.

seize jurisdiction he would become wicked in the act of doing so. The practice of hereditary kingship proved no obstacle to the need for consent for, if licit, it had to be based on an original act of consent to the whole dynasty. In the whole universe, only God held ruling power absolutely, in and of himself.[33]

Hervaeus applied his doctrine of consent both to the establishment of a ruling office and to the installation of a particular ruler. In both cases similar arguments applied. It was inherently fitting that a ruling office be established in any community because men needed government - here Hervaeus quoted Aristotle's *Politics* - and that a particular person of superior qualifications be appointed to the office. But the actual conferral of power on either office or person could come only from consent of the people, unless God himself bestowed power directly. 'No community can be justly obliged except by its own consent', Hervaeus wrote, 'or by command of one having lordship over it'.[34] But if the one having lordship ruled by mere force his rule was illicit. If he had been appointed to office by a licit superior then one had to ask where the superior got his jurisdiction from, and so on up through the hierarchy of command until in the end, if the whole system were licit, one would reach a person whose authority was based on consent. If we pressed such an enquiry through the ranks of the ecclesiastical hierarchy we should finally come to the pope. But the papacy was an elective office. The pope was chosen by the cardinals and the cardinals acted on behalf of the whole Christian community, which had entrusted to them the right of election. Hence the pope ruled by consent.[35] Once the head of a society was so established by general consent he could appoint a hierarchy of inferior governors who derived their authority from him (and so indirectly from consent).

Thus, as regards the person of the ruler, the doctrine of consent held universally; in secular government the doctrine applied to both the person and office of the ruler; but in the church, in the one case of the papacy, the ruling office was established directly by God. The rest of Hervaeus's argument was devoted to proving - against the defenders of episcopal autonomy - that the papacy was the only office in the church possessing a jurisdiction that was divinely ordained. He had no more to say about the rights of the ecclesiastical community except at one point - the same point that had troubled the canonists. A divinely established office ought to be infallible; but in fact popes as individuals could err. Hervaeus replied that they did not err when they followed the counsel of the whole universal church and that if a pope erred as an individual the church would not accept his decision, would not be 'obliged' by it.[36] Here again we find a recurring presumption of divine right, divine guidance inhering in the whole community.

[33] *De iur.*, pp. 16-17.
[34] *De pot.*, p. 364. *De iur.*, p. 16.
[35] *De iur.*, p. 17. On the role of the cardinals see also *De iur.*, p. 22. The one exception was Peter, who was instituted immediately by Christ.
[36] *De pot.*, p. 365.

Hervaeus cannot be called a constitutionalist. He was interested in defending a system of ecclesiology that a modern writer might call democratic centralism. But on the way to reaching that conclusion he provided a significant contribution to the growth of consent theory.

Another idiosyncratic theory of consent was developed at this time in the treatise *De legibus,* attributed, perhaps mistakenly, to Durandus of St Pourçain.[37] The author proceeded from a rather Hobbesian view of human nature to an overtly utilitarian theory of government. By nature men were inclined to pursue their own lusts without restraint, he wrote. If judges were not established they would at once go to war with one another.[38] But no natural order of government existed among men. 'The constituting of a ruler is a civil act, not a natural one', the author explained.[39] It was moreover an act based solely on considerations of expediency.

Let us suppose, the author argued, that there did exist one man in the world superior in wisdom to all the others. It would be fitting that he be honored; but he would not have a natural title to rule over all. For although this one man might have more knowledge about how to direct the community than any other individual, he could not have more knowledge than the whole community including himself. So by nature the right to rule always inhered in the whole community; but it was expedient to transfer the power to a particular ruler because the whole community could not easily meet together, and if it did, it would not easily agree. Since the transfer of power to a ruler was made solely for reasons of public expediency, it could be revoked when public expediency so dictated.[40]

On these foundations the author built a very utilitarian theory of positive law. 'Civil law does not take the nature of things as its foundation', he wrote, 'but rather public expediency, so that public expediency is the whole cause of establishing its conclusions.'[41] In the sphere of criminal law, for instance, there could be no question of the judge's considering the just deserts of an offender; he had to consider only public expediency. Thus it was often expedient to hang thieves; but in a society with an abundance of goods and a shortage of manpower it might not be expedient to do so, and the judge should act accordingly.[42] The author applied this principle over a whole range of social policies - marriage law, poor relief, property distribution. The argument seems starkly rationalistic. But theological premises were always lurking in the background.

---

[37] *Tractatus de Legibus* (Paris, 1506). For a fuller discussion see my paper, 'Public Expediency and Natural Law', in B. Tierney and P. Linehan (eds.), *Authority and Power. Studies on Medieval Law and Government Presented to Walter Ullmann on his Seventieth Birthday* (Cambridge, 1980), pp. 298-330. Durandus's authorship was denied by J. Koch. For discussion of this see 'Public Expediency', p. 169.

[38] fol. 12rb.   [41] fol. 10va.

[39] fol. 13vb.   [42] fols. 16va, 17ra.

[40] fol. 13vb.

The author doubted whether men would ever have formed governments to restrain their selfish wills at all, except for fear of divine retribution.[43] He held that, although men were bound only by a human law based on utilitarian considerations before human courts, they were always bound by natural law before God. Punishments awarded by human judges had to be based solely on public expediency; but God would be a true punisher in the next world.[44] The author insisted that, by divine will, individual property rights existed in natural law before the constituting of civil government;[45] but he also insisted that the civil law of property had to be based entirely on public expediency, not on the pre-existing natural rights.[46] To discuss all this would take us too far from our central theme of consent - but this rather odd work can remind us that all the arguments from utility, as well as from nature, that influenced the formulation of consent doctrine in the age of Hobbes and Locke were already beginning to surface early in the fourteenth century.

So far I have mentioned only in passing the best known of all the medieval consent theorists, Marsilius of Padua. It is evidently an exaggeration to describe his work, in the words of Ewart Lewis, as 'the first systematic statement of the popular basis of authority'. In arguing for consent as the basis of legitimacy, Marsilius was typical of a whole group of early fourteenth-century thinkers who were concerned with the problem of political obligation. But Marsilius certainly applied consent theory in an exceptionally broad-ranging fashion to both secular and ecclesiastical government. His major work, the *Defensor pacis*, contained two main sections: Discourse I dealt with the state, Discourse II with the church.[47] The underlying purpose of the book was to attack the theocratic claims of the papacy; and like other authors with the same objective Marsilius found it necessary to explain at the outset how licit jurisdiction could arise without papal authorization. He argued therefore that normally 'God . . . establishes government by means of human minds.' Then, purporting to expound Aristotle, Marsilius wrote: 'every government is over voluntary or involuntary subjects. The first is the genus of well-tempered governments.'[48] (But Aristotle really taught that the well-tempered governments were those that sought the common good.) In discussing the creation of law, Marsilius explained that law included both a discernment of what was just and a coercive command to obey. Any wise man could discern the just, but only the whole community, or its weightier part, could authorize coercive sanctions since a state was by definition 'a com-

---

[43] fol. 19rb.
[44] fol. 16va.
[45] fol. 14rb.
[46] fol. 14va-vb.
[47] C. W. Previté-Orton (ed.), *The Defensor Pacis of Marsilius of Padua* (Cambridge, 1928). A. Gewirth (trans.), *Marsilius of Padua. The Defender of the Peace*, II, *The Defensor pacis* (New York, 1956).
[48] 1.9.2, 5. Previté-Orton, pp. 30, 33; Gewirth, pp. 29, 31. (Marsilius presented Aristotle's view more accurately at 1.8.2.)

munity of free men'.[49] In an analogous argument, Marsilius asserted also that the 'efficient cause of the ruler' was 'the authority of . . . the whole body of citizens or the weightier part thereof'.[50]

Modern historians of political theory have concentrated mainly on these propositions of Discourse I. Some have found them 'revolutionary'. But these arguments did not evoke any great interest or criticism among Marsilius's contemporaries. The distinction between natural wisdom and coercive authority, the argument for coercive sanction as a necessary attribute of law, the emphasis on consent as the sole basis of legitimate government can all be found in earlier thinkers, and all these ideas had already been brought together in a coherent synthesis by Hervaeus Natalis.

It was Discourse II, dealing with the structure of the church, three times as long as Discourse I, argued with passion and fury, that formed the essential subject of the book for Marsilius himself and that outraged contemporary fourteenth-century opinion. A recurring paradox of Western thought is that ideas originally presented to justify an established order of things often prove to have revolutionary implications, when they are taken over by critics of the existing order. So it was with the doctrine of consent. Marsilius combined elements of Hervaeus's pro-papal consent theory with a variety of earlier criticisms of absolute papal power in such a way as to reach radical and novel conclusions. A reader familiar with the tangled undergrowth of medieval polemical pamphlets will recognize the sources of many of his ideas. With a sort of care-free eclecticism Marsilius took up the arguments of the episcopalists at the University of Paris who insisted that all the apostles, not Peter alone, received authority from Christ, and also the arguments of the most radical Franciscans (natural enemies of the episcopalists) who inveighed against the external wealth and coercive power of the church as a violation of the primitive Christian ideal. Marsilius exaggerated both sets of arguments, boldly combined them, and reached the very personal conclusions that Christ had not created an office of papal headship at all or bestowed coercive jurisdiction on any ecclesiastical prelate.[51]

According to Marsilius, Peter received from Christ the same office as the other apostles, but this was simply an office of teaching and administering sacraments. The only jurisdiction conferred on the church by divine command was a power to excommunicate, and this power inhered in the whole community of the faithful. It was granted, Marsilius asserted, by Christ's words at Matthew 18. 15-18: 'If your brother sin against you . . . go tell it to the church.'[52] This understanding of the text was not novel in itself. The canonists had occasionally referred to Mat-

---

[49] I.10.4, I.12.3, 6. Previté-Orton, pp. 38, 49, 52; Gewirth, pp. 36, 45, 47.
[50] I.15.1-2. Previté-Orton, p. 66; Gewirth, p. 61.
[51] 2.4.1, 2.16.1-19. Previté-Orton, pp. 128, 273-88; Gewirth, pp. 113, 241-53.
[52] 2.6.12-13. Previté-Orton, pp. 168-73; Gewirth, pp. 149-52.

thew 18.17 in their discussions on the denunciation of an erring pope. John of Paris too noted that 'power to coerce in the external forum' was conferred by these words of Christ.[53] But earlier writers had held that, even if Christ conferred jurisdiction on the whole church at Matthew 18.18, he also appointed Peter and the apostles (and their successors) to exercise that jurisdiction. Marsilius gave an unusually populist flavor to the text by asserting that, since jurisdiction inhered in the whole body of believers, and since Christ himself had instituted no office with coercive power, jurisdiction could be exercised only through offices and persons that derived their authority from the whole Christian community.

The *Defensor pacis* is a complex work and difficult to evaluate. Marsilius was bitterly anti-clerical and he may have been a religious sceptic; but if so he was probably driven to scepticism by the betrayal - or apparent betrayal - by a worldly church of an evangelical ideal of community consensus that continued to inform his writing. In extolling the virtues of the community or of a council representing it he went beyond what was necessary to sustain his attack on the papacy - as when he wrote that the decisions of general councils were decisions of the Holy Spirit and so, in matters of faith, immutably and infallibly true.[54] Occasionally a reflection of this enthusiasm appears in the more coolly argued Discourse I, as when he called the efficient cause of the state 'the spirit of the whole body of the citizens'.[55] One should note that the doctrines of consent supposedly derived from Aristotle in Discourse I do not exist in Aristotle. But they do exist in the Scriptural and patristic and canonistic authorities so copiously cited in Discourse II. The most common judgment of Marsilius is that he devised a rational theory of consent for the state and then applied it to the church. It seems at least as likely that he began from an ecclesiological doctrine of community consensus and then generalized it into a political theory.[56] If so he was rather typical. A great deal of subsequent consent theory would purport to be based on purely rational arguments, while resting really on theological premises that were concealed or unconsciously presupposed.

With William of Ockham, the last fourteenth-century theorist to be considered here, the concern with theology was quite overt. All Ockham's writing on political philosophy stemmed from a quarrel with the papacy about the true nature of the church. The dispute began over the Franciscan doctrine of evangelical poverty, then broadened to include the whole field of ecclesiology and political theory. Here I want to mention

---

[53] Bleienstein, p. 135; Watt, p. 153.
[54] 2.19.2-3, 2.20.8. Previté-Orton, pp. 312-14, 323; Gewirth, 274-5, 283.
[55] 1.15.6. Previté-Orton, p. 70; Gewirth, p. 64.
[56] More commonly Marsilius's attitude has been related to the corporate life of the Italian cities. But there is not really an either/or argument here. No doubt various influences contributed to his thought. The ecclesiological dimension should not be neglected (as Gordon Leff has observed).

IV

Popular sovereignty, federalism, and fundamental law: Azo to Althusius

In this lecture I want to discuss some stages in the development of the interrelated ideas that I have called 'popular sovereignty', 'federalism', and 'fundamental law' from the thirteenth century to the seventeenth. The argument begins with some scattered remarks of the Roman lawyer, Azo, and ends with the complex synthesis of Althusius. In between, the fifteenth-century conciliarists had shaped theories of church government that (as Figgis long ago pointed out) would eventually prove applicable to political societies in general.

Let us introduce the subject with some words from a founder of modern federalism. James Madison wrote: 'A dependence on the people is no doubt the primary control on government; but experience has taught mankind the necessity of auxiliary precautions.' The 'auxiliary precautions' have often included a diffusion of authority designed to prevent any one man from wielding absolute despotic power, and a structure of constitutional law intended to bind the government itself. The diffusion of authority can take many forms, described in phrases that had become common by the seventeenth century as 'double sovereignty', 'dual majesty', 'mixed government', 'mixed monarchy', 'limited monarchy'. Anyone who has studied Gierke's sometimes sibylline utterances on these matters will know how complex they can become. But there are two broad patterns of diffusion that commonly recur: a diffusion of authority between central government and local governments regulated by a fundamental law, a system of 'federalism'; and diffusion of authority within the central government itself, a system of 'checks and balances'. The two systems are not mutually exclusive of course; the American constitution combines both. But they are conceptually distinguishable and they provide helpful categories for exploring the intricacies of modern constitutional thought or, at any rate, the origins of those intricacies. In the present discussion we shall be concerned mainly with the first type of diffusion, the 'federalist' pattern.

Some defenders of constitutional government, especially English ones, have always maintained that unitary sovereignty is essential to the coherence of a state. This raises obvious difficulties for theorists of federalism,

just two issues raised in the *Dialogus,* where Ockham seems to have pressed consent theory a little further than his contemporaries.

The fourteenth-century authors we have considered so far perceived that innate superiority did not in itself confer jurisdiction - rather, consent of the community did - but they all assumed that the head of a community had to possess exceptional qualities, and they favored elective procedures in part because they thought that election was most likely to produce an outstanding ruler. Marsilius, for instance, observed that 'by the method of election alone is the best ruler obtained'.[57] Ockham, discussing the election of a pope, chose to consider the difficult situation that would arise if no outstanding man were available. In pursuing the question, he argued at length that a legitimate ruler could be constituted out of a group of equals by an act of sheer will. A modern critic has noted that Hobbes's sovereign did not possess more reason than other men nor acquire more by his election. 'All that was artificial about the sovereign was his power to command.' Ockham's argument points in the same direction; and for him too utilitarian considerations were decisive. He began from Aristotle's observation that a monarch ought not to rule permanently over subjects unless he were as superior to them as gods and heroes to ordinary men. Ockham argued against this opinion from both Scripture and utility. St Peter was not more holy than the other apostles, he pointed out - indeed he was inferior to St Paul in wisdom and to St John in love - yet he was made head of the church. Similarly Saul was inferior to Samuel in virtue, but Saul was made king. Aristotle's doctrine held good, Ockham argued, only when we considered merely the merits of the one receiving honor; but in fact it was necessary also to consider public utility. The doctrine that equal honor be given to equals was valid only so long as it was convenient and useful. If the common good so required it was fitting that one man be raised above others who were his equals. Arguably it was better to have any sort of head than no head at all.[58]

Ockham followed this argument by raising another difficult point for discussion. Could the congregation of the faithful change the form of government originally established in the church? Could the community, for instance, decide to substitute an aristocracy for papal monarchy? Here again Ockham was touching on a theme that became of central importance in later constitutional thought - the doctrine that a community possessed an inalienable right, not precisely a right to govern but a right to constitute government, and not merely a right to establish a ruler but a right to change the accepted form of government without dissolving the community itself. Moreover, he was considering the extreme case of

[57] 1.9.7. Previté-Orton, p. 34; Gewirth, p. 33.
[58] *Dialogus,* in M. Goldast, *Monarchia S. Romani Imperii,* II (Frankfurt, 1614), 3.1.2.13-17, pp.798-803.

changing a form of government originally established by God. Ockham argued that the congregation of the faithful, more than any other society, was endowed with everything needed for its own well-being; but it would not be optimally endowed if it lacked the power to change its own form of rule when this became expedient. Papal monarchy had been established in the church for reasons of 'common utility'; if this form of government ceased to be useful, it should cease to exist. The argument against all this of course was that the legitimate form of constitution for the church had been laid down once and for all in Scripture. But Ockham suggested that, for reasons of evident utility or necessity, it was permitted to go against Scripture in matters that were morally indifferent. The argument ended inconclusively (like all the arguments in the *Dialogus*) but it is interesting as an example of the range of speculation we encounter in fourteenth-century thought on legitimacy and consent.[59]

It has recently been argued that 'a drastic alteration in the fundamental assumptions of political thought' occurred in the seventeenth century, because then 'individual liberty and equality . . . were employed to combat the ideas of status, hierarchy, and degree which had satisfied and justified the medieval social order'.[60] But this is at best an oversimplification. The theory of government by consent (based on arguments from liberty and equality) was fully formulated by the early fourteenth century; the practice of government by hierarchy, status, and degree continued to flourish in the seventeenth. However, although medieval authors established the foundations for much later consent theory, they left some questions unanswered - the kind of questions that critics of the doctrine of consent would raise in the seventeenth century and that modern students of political theory still raise. The most difficult problems concern the nature of human will itself. If the will can choose either good or evil, how can a mere act of will - consent - establish a licit regime? A commonsensical argument going back to Aristotle asserts that many heads are wiser than one; but is there any sense in which many wills are better than one? Another set of problems arises in considering the ways in which consent can be expressed. Is a bare numerical majority always adequate? Does mere tacit consent suffice? And, if so, how is the existence of tacit consent to be inferred? We shall touch on some of these points in later discussions. But another consideration is more immediately important if one is considering consent in relation to the development of constitutional thought as a whole. The doctrine of consent is essential to all theories of constitutional government; but it can also serve as a basis for absolutist theories. Every modern dictator claims to rule by consent and some of them presumably do so. Hervaeus Natalis favored centralized papal monarchy in the church. Marsilius of Padua, according

to many modern scholars, upheld an absolutist theory of the state. Constitutionalism requires not only consent to rulership but also limitations on the powers of rulers. The next two lectures will explore some of the ways in which theories of limited government came to be formulated.

---

[59] *Dialogus* 3.1.2.20-2, pp. 806-10.
[60] D. W. Hanson, *From Kingdom to Commonwealth* (Cambridge, Mass., 1970), p. 337.

especially American ones. Americans see federalism and fundamental law as of the very essence of constitutionalism; they also see the English constitutional tradition as the principal ancestor of their own; but, exasperatingly, English government knows neither fundamental constitutional law nor federalism. This worries American scholars. Some years ago Professor Goodhart insisted that the English really do have a fundamental law which they understand perfectly well even though they refuse to define it for other people. More heroically, Professor McIlwain once claimed to discern the origins of American federalism in the constitutional structure of the British Isles during the seventeenth century - he waxed eloquent on the precise status of the Isle of Man. There is perhaps more to be said for Goodhart than for McIlwain here. Possibly the English do have such a deep intuitive understanding of fundamental law that they have never felt a need to articulate that understanding; certainly they have no intuitive understanding of federalism. In the dominant English tradition the simplistic doctrine of parliamentary sovereignty has to cover all contingencies.

English experience points to a real problem here; a theory of sovereignty and a practice of federalism have always been hard to reconcile. The fact was clearly apparent in 1786. When a federal constitution for the United States was proposed, anti-Federalists derided the whole enterprise. They could not imagine 'a sovereignty of power existing within a sovereign power'. 'Two co-ordinate sovereignties . . . would be contrary to the very nature of things', they argued. The Federalists found an effective answer to all this only when they asserted that an ultimate, inalienable sovereignty inhered in the whole people. Granted that, then as James Wilson wrote, 'They can delegate it . . . to such bodies, on such terms, and under such limitations as they think proper.'[1]

Federalism has been defined as a system 'in which two levels of government operate within the same geographical limits and neither has the power to destroy the other',[2] implying, of course, that the power of the regional government is not just a delegation from the central one. It is perhaps logically impossible to construct such a system without postulating a sovereign above and beyond any specific organ of government; and this sovereign can only be the people or, if federalism is to be defended within a theological framework of thought, 'God through the people'. There must always then be a populist element in federalism. But there must always be a pluralist element too. It is not enough for the people to

[1] Gordon S. Wood, *The Creation of the American Republic, 1776-1787* (Chapel Hill, 1969), p. 530.

[2] J. P. Roche, 'Constitutional Law', in *International Encyclopedia of the Social Sciences* (New York, 1968), III, 300-17 (p. 301), referring to K. C. Wheare. Federalism has come to mean much more than this of course, but an approach on the level of intergovernmental relations seems most appropriate in a study on constitutional thought. The best brief guide to modern literature in the field is S. Rufus Davis, *The Federal Principle* (Berkeley-Los Angeles, 1978).

delegate power; they must delegate it on at least two levels, central and local.

In the seventeenth century, the political thinkers who were really concerned about problems of federalism were not Englishmen but those Europeans who had to deal with the structure of the Dutch Republic or the German Empire - Grotius, Pufendorf, and above all Althusius. One modern authority had called Althusius 'the real father of modern federal theory'. Carl Friedrich adds that 'a very definite road leads from Althusius . . . to American institutions, especially federalism'.[3] If there is such a road, no one has succeeded in tracing its course, and it lies outside our boundaries. But there is another road that begins in the legal and ecclesiological thought of the thirteenth century and wends its way to a termination in Althusius. This road we will try to explore. We will begin with some aspects of medieval populist theory, then turn back to examine the pluralist doctrines of church structure presented by certain thirteenth-century theologians, and finally consider how the two strands of thought became interwoven in the work of Nicholas of Cues and in the truly federalist system of Althusius.

POPULISM: RULER AND COMMUNITY

I am consistently using the word 'populism' in a special sense (but one that seems philologically justified) to designate the theory that sovereignty always resides inalienably in the *populus*, the whole people, even after the institution of a government. In the real-life world of the thirteenth century this sentiment was nourished by the intense communal experience of the growing cities, especially in Italy. The idea could also be derived from the canonists' teaching that only the whole church was indefectible in faith, so that in a sense the church, the congregation of the faithful, was always superior to any of its ministers. But the most explicit formulation of the theory of inalienable popular sovereignty at this time came from certain of the Roman lawyers, and among them Azo provided the most coherent presentation of the doctrine.

The discussions of the civilians usually began from a text of the *Digest*. 'Laws themselves are binding because the people accept them . . . hence laws are abrogated not only by the voice of the legislator but also by the fact of their falling out of use by common consent.' It seemed that, if the people chose to pursue a custom contrary to existing law, then the custom of the people would prevail. On the other hand, another well-known passage of the *Digest* declared, 'What has pleased the Prince has the force of law . . . since the people conferred all its imperium and power on him.'[4] The apparent conflict was more important for medieval jurists than

---

[3] D. J. Elarzar, 'Federalism', in *International Encyclopedia . . .*, v, 353-67 (p. 363). C. J. Friedrich, *Politica methodica digesta of Johannes Althusius* (Cambridge, Mass., 1932) (reprint of the 3rd edn of 1614), p. xix.

[4] *Dig.* 1.3.32, 1.4.1.

for the original compilers of the *Digest* simply because so much of the medieval law in day-to-day use was based on popular custom (custom that was often quite consciously created, as we have noted). In an attempt to reconcile the two texts, some civilians argued that the first one referred only to the period before the people established a ruler. Thus, in the twelfth century, Rogerius and Placentinus described the emperor as a 'minister' or 'vicar' of the people but both held none the less that, once an emperor was established, the people lost its power to institute or abrogate law. Hugolinus, on the other hand, asserted that, since the emperor was only a 'proctor' acting on behalf of the people, they retained their own intrinsic authority after his election.[5]

This was also the view of Azo. The people *conceded* power; they did not *transfer* it in the sense of alienating it from themselves, Azo wrote, using language that would be repeated endlessly in later political theory. Accordingly the people retained power to make law or abrogate law even after the institution of an emperor. Commenting on a text of the Code which attributed to 'the emperor alone' the right to make law, Azo explained that the word 'alone' applied only to other individuals, not to the corporate body of the people - 'Individuals are excluded, not the *universitas*.' This seems to lead on to a particularly awkward form of the doctrine that later would be called 'double sovereignty'. (Some political theorists came to hold that sovereignty inhered in both the ruler and the people; others pointed out that attributing sovereignty to one party necessarily excluded the other.) In Azo's formulation both the emperor and the people had a right to institute binding laws, perhaps contradictory ones. But Azo probably intended to argue for the ultimate sovereignty of the people, for he held that in the last resort they possessed a right to depose the ruler whom they had instituted.[6]

This still leaves us with the paradox we mentioned in an earlier discussion. How could an emperor be at once set above the people and subordinate to them; or, as a seventeenth-century author put it, 'If the people shall be governors, who shall be the governed?' Here again medieval jurists found an answer in the Roman law theory of corporations. Such a response was already suggested by Irnerius, the first great medieval glossator of Roman law. 'The people command as a *universitas*; they promise and engage [to obey] as individuals.'[7] Azo expressed the same idea in a classical formulation that would find many adaptions and appli-

---

[5] Many relevent texts are conveniently assembled in R. W. and A. J. Carlyle, *Political Theory*, II, *The Political Theory of the Roman Lawyers and the Canonists* (Edinburgh-London, 1909). On Rogerius, Placentinus, and Hugolinus see pp. 58-67. See also Cortese, *La norma*, II, 174-7. The canonists carried on a parallel debate all through the later Middle Ages, usually starting out from a dictum of Gratian at *Dist.* 4 p.c.3, 'Laws are instituted when they are promulgated; they are confirmed when they are approved by the practice of those using them.' On these discussions see L. de Lucca, 'L'accettazione popolare della legge canonica nel pensiero di Graziano e dei sui interpreti', *Studia Gratiana*, 3 (1955), 193-276.

[6] Azo, *Summa Codicis ad* 1.14.8, 1.14.12. Carlyle, pp. 64-5; Cortese, pp. 175-6.

[7] Gloss *and Dig.* 1.3.1. Carlyle, p. 57.

cations among later writers. 'The emperor does not have more power than the whole people but than each individual of the people.'[8] And since Azo held that the people could depose the emperor, he was really attributing more power to the people than to the ruler. This was not a matter of mere arithmetic, that there were a lot of people and only one emperor. The distinction was between the people considered as a corporate body – a *universitas* – and the people considered as a mass of individuals. Azo explained the difference further in his *Summa* on *Cod.* 3. 13, where he presented the doctrine that a *universitas*, but not a collection of separate individuals, could create a judge possessing ordinary jurisdiction; and again in his *Lectura* on *Cod.* 1.14.8 where he discussed in considerable detail the delictal responsibilities of corporations (as distinct from those of the individuals who composed them).

For Azo then the emperor was less than the corporate body of the people but greater than the individuals who composed it. Jacques de Révigny stated this doctrine more extremely in the later thirteenth century. It was not only that the Roman people had not in fact alienated their jurisdiction; in principle it was impossible for them to do so. 'Even if they wanted to relinquish it they could not', wrote Jacques, and he added, 'The people has no superior; it is true that the emperor is superior to each one of the people, but he is not superior to the people.'[9]

This view, however, was always a minority one among Roman lawyers, and in the early fourteenth century Cynus of Pistoia dismissed the whole argument as a kind of irrelevant antiquarianism. He told his students, 'You may hold the opinion that pleases you best . . . I don't care. For I know that if in fact the Roman people should establish a law or custom no one would observe it outside the city.' Bartolus took a similar position. Although he wrote strongly in favor of popular government in other contexts, he regarded this particular dispute as irrelevant to the circumstances of his own world.

Then, when Azo's doctrine seemed to be falling out of favor altogether, it was revised in a new form as a principle of ecclesiology. In the crisis of the Great Schism, when there were two contending 'popes' and no individual judge set over them, it seemed essential to affirm again the underlying authority of the whole church. For a canonist, the most obvious way to do this was to assert that the mystical body of the church, like a legal corporation, was capable of sustaining its own unfailing corporate life whatever vicissitudes might befall its head. In 1408 Cardinal Zabarella combined this argument from corporation law with the populist doctrine stemming from the *Digest*. 'The pope has plenitude of

[8]   Azo, *Lectura ad Cod.* 8.53.2. Cortese, p. 176.
[9]   For Révigny and other fourteenth-century jurists see W. Ullmann, *The Medieval Idea of Law as Represented by Lucas de Penna* (London, 1946), pp. 48–51. (Révigny's work was mistakenly attributed to Petrus de Bellapertica by the sixteenth-century editor.) The texts of Cynus and Bartolus are discussed in C. N. S. Woolf, *Bartolus of Sassoferrato* (Cambridge, 1913), pp. 37, 40. (All three jurists were commenting on *Cod.* 1.14.12.)

power', he wrote, 'not as an individual but as head of a corporation so that the power is in the corporate whole as its foundation and in the pope as the principal minister through whom it is exercised.' Then he added that, just as the Roman people had not alienated its own inherent authority in instituting an emperor, so the church did not alienate its authority in electing a pope.[10] In 1409, Ludolf of Sagan argued that, although the pope could not be judged by any individual, he could be judged by the corporate body - the *universitas* - of the church.[11] This is a variant of Azo's Roman law doctrine, but the argument has undergone a shift of meaning in being applied to the church. Azo had in mind the people of the city of Rome, who could actually assemble together. Ludolf was thinking of the general council as a representative body acting on behalf of the whole church. Later conciliar writers often asserted that the pope was sovereign over individual members of the dispersed church but not over the corporate whole assembled in a council.

In 1415 the Council of Constance actually claimed supreme authority for itself as representing the church. 'This holy synod . . . representing the Catholic church militant, holds power immediately from Christ and anyone of whatsoever state or dignity, even if it be the papal, is bound to obey it.' The council subsequently removed all three contending pontiffs and prepared to elect a new pope of unity. At this point the problem of 'double sovereignty' arose in a new form. The council had claimed power for itself at a time when there was no certainly legitimate pope. But what would happen when one was elected? Would he somehow share sovereignty with the council? A pro-papal spokesman, Leonard Statius, argued that, although jurisdiction as such inhered always in the church, once a new pope was elected the actual exercise of jurisdiction would belong entirely to him and not to the council at all. This was to divide sovereignty in a way that gave all real power to the ruler. An anonymous conciliar spokesman, vehemently attacking Statius's position, argued for a unitary sovereignty inhering in the community. There could be only one supreme power, he argued. To postulate two supreme powers - one in the church and one in the pope - was logically absurd. The one supreme power must inhere in the council. It could not be divided between pope and council because they might oppose and frustrate one another. It could not reside in the pope because the council could depose the pope and not vice versa. The speaker concluded with another variation on the populist theme: 'The pope can judge individuals . . . but he cannot judge the whole church.'[12]

10 *Tractatus de schismate,* in Schardius, *De iurisdictione . . . imperiali ac potestate ecclesiastica* (Basle, 1566), pp. 688-711 (pp. 703, 708).
11 *Tractatus,* ed. J. Loserth, in *Archiv für Österreichische Geschichte,* 60 (Vienna, 1880), 343-561 (p. 555).
12 H. Finke, *Acta Concilii Constanciensis,* 11 (Münster, 1923), 705-29 (p. 729). For further discussion see my ' "Divided Sovereignty" at Constance: A Problem of Medieval and Early Modern Political Theory', *Annuarium historiae conciliorum,* 7 (1975), 238-56.

Similar views were often expressed at the Council of Basle in the 1430s. Andreas Escobar specifically applied to the church the old Roman law argument: 'The power of the people is greater than the power of their rulers . . . because they could not alienate jurisdiction from themselves.'[13] John of Segovia argued that a ruler was greater than any individual or particular group in his community since he represented them all as a 'public person', but that the whole community assembled together was of greater authority than the ruler.[14] Alfonso Garcia, bishop of Burgos, delivered a lengthy speech in which, we are told, he moved from 'divine and human law' to Aristotelian political theory to theological exegesis of the Petrine texts of Scripture. In the course of his oration Garcia declared: 'For a king to have more power than the whole of the kingdom is absurd; therefore the pope should not have more power than the Church.' The pope, he argued, was beneath a council though greater than all individual Christians.[15]

Speeches, like books, have their fates. In this case the bishop's views were recorded by Aenius Sylvius Piccolomini in his history of the Council of Basle and passed from there to various Protestant works of political theory. (William Prynne quoted Garcia directly in his *Soveraigne Power of Parliaments*.) In the influential *Vindiciae contra tyrannos* the bishop's argument was reversed. The author wrote that, just as a general council was superior to a pope, so the assembled estates of a realm could depose its king. Elsewhere he added the explanation that by then had become a commonplace: 'As all the whole people is above the King, and likewise taken in one entire body, are in authority before him, yet being considered one by one, they are all of them under the King.'[16]

PLURALISM: POPE AND BISHOPS

So far we have traced some roots of a populist theory of sovereignty. But we have not yet discussed the 'pluralism' which was an essential ingredient in early modern theories of federalism. In fact all the major conciliar thinkers were in a sense 'pluralist' in their theories of church government. That is to say they believed that each bishop held an authority which was not derived from the pope but from the fundamental constitution of the church itself or, as John of Paris wrote, 'from God and the people'. To understand this pluralist, episcopalist element in conciliar thought - and it was a central element - we must go back and explore another tradition of medieval ecclesiology.

Historians of federalism sometimes begin with the twelve tribes of

---

[13] A. J. Black, *Monarchy and Community: Political Ideas in the Later Conciliar Controversy 1430-1450* (Cambridge, 1970), p. 10.
[14] Black, p. 148.
[15] D. Hay and K. W. Smith (eds.), *De gestis Concilii Basiliensis commentariorum* (Oxford, 1967), pp. 29-35.
[16] Laski (ed.), *A Defense of Liberty*, pp. 127, 204-5.

Israel; they always mention ancient Greek and medieval Italian leagues of city-states; they glance at decentralized forms of feudalism, and even perhaps at medieval church-state conflicts; and they usually conclude that none of the power relationships they have explored really corresponds to those of federal thought, mainly because they lack an adequate doctrine of sovereignty. But this is to ignore a most important early chapter in the history of the doctrine – the debates between papalists and episcoplists about the right ordering of the church that began in Paris around 1250. The literature of these debates is very well known to students of medieval ecclesiology, but it has never received quite the attention it deserves in general histories of political thought.

The dispute of the 1250s was at bottom an episcopal reaction against the increasing centralization of power in the papacy. Its immediate cause was episcopal resentment against the new, papally sponsored orders of mendicant friars – especially the Franciscans and Dominicans. The friars, equipped with papal privileges, were able to enter parishes without permission of the local clergy, preach to the people, administer sacraments, hear confessions, collect offerings. In effect, the popes were using their sovereign authority as heads of the church to set up a new pastoral structure alongside the old one. Some theologians came to see this as subversive of all right order in the Christian community.[17]

Overt intellectual feuding began in 1252 at the University of Paris, where the secular masters of theology had their own grievances against the friars. The dispute took a new turn in 1256 when a Franciscan, Thomas of York, declared that one supreme hierarch existed in the church, the pope, from whom all power descended to lesser prelates; and that, accordingly, whatever privileges the pope granted to friars, bishops had no right to protest since all their own jurisdiction was derived from the papacy. This 'derivational' theory was not new in itself, but it had never been asserted so trenchantly and in such a sensitive context. In the explosive atmosphere of 1256 it transformed what had been a vague grumbling about the activities of the friars, based largely on the jealousy of the secular masters, into a great debate about the proper constitution of the church.

None of the episcopalists denied the doctrine of universal papal jurisdiction. Their first great spokesman, William of St Amour, acknowledged that the pope was 'highest of bishops and universal judge of everyone'.[18] It was precisely because they acknowledged the pope's sovereignty that they anticipated some of the ideas and problems of later federalism. For they did deny most emphatically that the pope was the source of their own jurisdiction; they maintained rather that papal headship was

---

[17] On the whole controversy see Y. M.-J. Congar, 'Aspects ecclésiologiques de la querelle entre mendiants et séculiers', *Archives d'histoire doctrinale et littéraire du moyen âge*, 36 (1961), 35-151.

[18] *Opera omnia* (Constance, 1632), p. 146. The quoted texts of William of St Amour are from his *De periculis* (*Opera*, pp. 17-72) and *Collationes catholicae* (*Opera*, pp. 111-487).

defined by a divinely established fundamental law of the church, which also attributed autonomous authority to each bishop in his own diocese. In his general attacks on the friars' way of life, William of St Amour displayed a remarkable gift for colorful invective and sustained irony. It would be entertaining to quote him at length in this vein but here we can consider only his relatively calm and sober arguments about the governance of the church. William was the very prototype of a conservative constitutionalist. Like many such, he was a little too inclined to attribute immemorial antiquity to those innovations of the recent past that he happened to find congenial; but often he was able to appeal with considerable effect against the papal policies he deplored to the ancient tradition of the church and especially to the constitutional law that he found in Gratian's *Decretum*. He relied above all on *Dist.* 21 c.2:

> In the New Testament, after Christ the sacerdotal order began from Peter . . . The other apostles indeed received honor and power with him in equal fellowship and they wanted him to be their leader . . . When they died bishops succeeded in their places . . . Also seventy-two disciples were chosen of whom priests are the image.

This text remained of central importance through all the later disputes. It is in fact from Pseudo-Isidore, a ninth-century forgery; but genuine patristic doctrine lies behind it. In particular, the teaching that the twelve apostles prefigured the order of bishops and the seventy-two disciples the order of priests goes back to Bede, and the teaching that all the apostles were called to a fellowship of equal honor and power with Peter goes back to Cyprian. Among his many references to the *Decretum*, William also cited *Dist.* 68 c.5, which again referred to the twelve and the seventy-two as the only orders instituted by Christ; and *Dist.* 99 c.5, where Pope Gregory I disdained the title of universal bishop; and *Causa* 25 q.1 c.6, which declared: 'If [the Roman pontiff] should seek to destroy what the apostles have taught . . . he is convicted of error'; [19] but if the pope maintained that the bishops were merely his delegates and if he tried to diminish their jurisdiction, William declared, he would indeed destroy the teaching of the apostles.

William's ecclesiology has been called 'feudal' because of his concern with local autonomy; and no doubt he was not really interested in popular rights. But since, as another author wrote, 'Christ does not come down from heaven' to appoint bishops,[20] William had to offer some kind of explanation for the immediate origins of episcopal authority. Hence he wrote that 'only those who are rightly elected are called by God' and that the rightly elected bishop was sent 'by God through man', again referring to the *Decretum*.[21]

William was in fact appealing to ancient constitutional law against an

---

[19] *Opera*, pp. 24, 145, 148-9.
[20] John de Pouilly, in J. G. Sikes, 'John de Pouilly and Peter de la Palu', *English Historical Review*, 49 (1934), 219-40 (p. 229 n.3).
[21] *Opera*, pp. 24, 144.

abuse of papal sovereignty - or what he conceived to be an abuse. He did not deny that the pope could send friars into a diocese to supplement the work of the parish priests if there was good reason in an individual case. But he did deny that the pope could issue a general license to an indeterminate number of friars to preach anywhere in the church without consent of the local clergy; for, he held, this would destroy the authority of the lower prelates and so upset the divinely established constitution of the church. William therefore repeatedly contended - or pretended - that the pope could not really have intended to grant such general licenses. Even Jesus had sent out only selected preachers whom he himself had taught. It was not likely that the lord pope would intend to abandon the example of Jesus. And St Paul had declared: 'No man should glory in another man's office.' It was not likely that the lord pope would intend to go against St Paul. And Gregory I had written, 'I do injury to myself if I disturb the rights of my brother [bishops].' It was not likely that the lord pope would intend to differ from St Gregory.[22] Since the lord pope quite obviously did intend precisely what William said he ought not to intend this was all a sort of polite insolence. The pope perceived it as such; he promptly condemned William's work and exiled him from Paris. William had to retire to his native village of St Amour. But he never recanted and he never ceased to write against the papal policies.

Meanwhile his ideas were carried on by a whole new generation of thinkers at Paris. The next major contribution was made by Gerard of Abbeville. He supplemented William's arguments, based mainly on canon law, with an additional dossier of scriptural and patristic texts. Gerard pointed out that Christ gave power not only to Peter but also to the twelve apostles at Luke 9.1-2 and to the seventy-two disciples at Luke 10.1. And that, when Christ said to Peter at Matthew 16.19, 'I will give you the keys of the kingdom of heaven', he did not speak to Peter alone; rather Peter symbolized the whole church. This view, well known to the canonists, derived from Augustine, as we saw. Gerard added to the authority of Augustine that of Cyprian, Athanasius, and Jerome in support of his interpretation. Moreover, he pointed out that at Matthew 18. 18 Christ spoke to all the twelve the words he had first said to Peter. 'Whatsoever you shall bind on earth it shall be bound in heaven.' And he said to them all at Matthew 28.19: 'Go and teach all nations.'[23] Christ had indeed designated Peter as head of the church to preserve unity, Gerard acknowledged, but he did not confer power on Peter alone; rather, 'he conferred on the others the same power of binding and loosing' that Peter received.[24] In effect Jesus had established for his church a pluralistic constitution. Each bishop was like a captain of his own little ship, Gerard explained, exercising the same authority over it that the pope did over the great ship that was the universal church.[25]

Gerard insisted that the pope could not change the church's constitution. To assert that episcopal power came from the pope (rather than from God) was to 'enervate the state of the whole church'. The pope's power was given for 'edification' not for 'destruction'; he could not use his power therefore to 'destroy the state of the church'.[26] We have seen that twelfth-century canonists used the words 'state of the church' when seeking to set a limit to papal power; but they never really explained what the phrase meant. From the late 1250s onward it could be used to designate a fundamental constitutional law, assigning a co-ordinate status to the bishops with the pope in the rule of the church and binding on the pope himself. In discussing the emergence of the secular idea of the state, Quentin Skinner has observed that the crucial change is 'from the idea of a ruler "maintaining his state" to the more abstract idea that there is an independent political apparatus, that of the State, which the ruler may be said to have a duty to maintain'.[27] A similar sort of development occurred in the sphere of ecclesiology during the thirteenth century.

The texts in which Christ granted or appeared to grant authority to some person or group in the church were of course endlessly scrutinized and reinterpreted from this time onward all through the Middle Ages and through the Reformation centuries too. (Extreme papalists usually came to emphasize John 21.15-17, 'Feed my lambs . . . feed my sheep', for these words clearly seemed addressed to Peter alone.) While the protagonists on both sides appealed mainly to the primeval constitution of the church as revealed in Scripture and canon law they also sometimes turned to arguments from natural reason. The Dominican, Peter of la Palu, after maintaining that the words 'Feed my sheep' conferred power on Peter alone, added that this interpretation had a rational basis because Aristotle had proved in the *Politics* that monarchy was the best form of government. William Godin preferred to quote Aristotle's *Metaphysics*. 'A plurality of rulers is not good as is shown in the *Metaphysics*';[28] therefore Christ could not have established twelve rulers in his church. Episcopalists like Henry of Ghent and John of Pouilli argued that it was against natural law to withdraw subjects from obedience to their normal rulers. All parties appealed to analogies with secular government.

Let us go back to our modern definition of federalism. 'A system in which two levels of government operate within the same geographical limits and neither has the power to destroy the other'. This was precisely the position of a thirteenth-century episcopalist. One can illustrate the

[25] p. 204, referring to Bernard of Clairvaux.
[26] pp. 200, 203.
[27] *Foundations of Modern Political Thought*, 1, p. x.
[28] *De causa immediata ecclesiastice potestatis* (Paris, 1506), fol. 11vb-12ra. For Peter de la Palu see Congar, 'Aspects ecclésiologiques', p. 98 n. 187.

point best perhaps from Godfrey of Fontaines, writing in the 1280s. The authority of bishops was not delegated by the pope, he wrote, but instituted directly by Christ. Whatever a pope could do a bishop could do 'simply and absolutely'. The difference was that a bishop's power was limited to his own diocese while a pope's extended universally over the whole church. The church was not just an undifferentiated mass of individuals, united only by adherence to a single head. Rather the church was a cluster of communities each under its own bishop. Godfrey wrote that, just as the church of Paris was a mystical body of many persons joined to its bishop as head and principal member, so all the churches formed a general unity, one community in which the local churches were joined to one another and to a ruling head and principal member who was the pope.[29] Two levels of government, one might say, operated within the same geographical limits - the local authority of the bishop and the universal authority of the pope. And the lower power was not derived from the higher. As for the second half of our definition, 'neither level can destroy the other', this was the whole point of the episcopalist argument. The French bishops did not imagine that they could destroy the papal power; but, they insisted, neither could the pope destroy theirs.

I suggested that this obscure tract of ecclesiology is important in the general history of constitutional thought. It is not only that the ideas are interesting in themselves. It is not only that the churchmen anticipated some very odd ways of thinking that will recur in secular writers - the appeal simultaneously to an ancient constitution and to natural reason, the suave refusal to admit that the monarch could really intend the policies carried out in his name. It is also that their ideas never died away. Most importantly for us, episcopalist doctrines formed an essential element in fifteenth-century conciliar theory and, through conciliarist writings, influenced much subsequent constitutional theory. But even after the conciliar movement had failed, the ideas of William of St Amour lived on in seventeenth-century theological Gallicanism, a movement that was still characterized, as a recent author has observed, by 'a certain bias towards constitutionalism' and by 'an assumption that the entire institutional order was pluralistic rather than unitary'.[30] (Indeed William's *Opera omnia* were first printed in Paris in 1632 - but in a clandestine edition. After four centuries William was still too provocative to publish openly.) From the thirteenth century to the seventeenth, whatever other constitutional squabbles arose, this one was always going on in the background, a fundamental dispute about the right ordering of the Catholic church.

---

29 *Quodlibetales* 13 q.5, in J. Hoffmans (ed.), *Les philosophes belges,* v (Louvain, 1932), 223.

30 W. Bowsma, 'Gallicanism and the Nature of Christendom', in A. Molho (ed.), *Renaissance Studies in Honor of Hans Baron* (De Kalb, 1971), pp. 811-30. Bowsma associated these characteristics with the legal background of many Gallican spokesmen.

NICHOLAS OF CUES

During the conciliar epoch the most impressive synthesis of the various ideas we have considered so far was presented in the *De concordantia catholica* of Nicholas of Cues, written at the Council of Basle in 1432.[31] Although Nicholas's work has been discussed so often, it may be rewarding to look at it once more from a slightly different point of view, specifically as an exemplification of the two principal traditions of thought we have been exploring - 'populism', the idea that the whole community, by virtue of its inalienable sovereignty, remains superior to any office of government within it; and 'pluralism', the idea that the inherent authority of the community can be distributed to different levels of government in accordance with a preordained fundamental law.

Figgis gave a couple of pages to Nicholas of Cues and observed that the title of his *Concordantia* might remind us of Gratian's *Concord of Discordant Canons*. But he did not notice, or at least did not state, that this was no mere coincidence. Cusanus was indeed a professional canonist. He would have spent several years studying Gratian's *Decretum* or *Concordantia*, and his own work is filled with references to Gratian's texts. It is an extraordinary attempt to build a new structure out of the old materials, to combine in a harmonious synthesis the neo-Platonic idea that all power descends from above with the view that licit authority derives from the people; to combine a doctrine of papal headship with an assertion of episcopal autonomy; and in doing these things to formulate general principles of government that would apply to both ecclesiastical and secular regimes.

Nicholas's characteristic doctrine, the one that gave coherence to his whole work, was an assertion that the divine will expressed itself in human affairs through community consent or consensus. This explained, in the first place, the origin of all legitimate authority. 'All power, which is primarily from God, is judged divine when it arises from a common concord of the subjects.'[32] The idea that a ruler's authority could come from God through the people was common enough by this time, but Nicholas presented it with a new wealth of metaphor and a new range of applications. In discussing church government, he wrote that all power was latent in the community but that, for actual rulership to emerge, a 'form-giving radiance' from above was required.[33] Nicholas sometimes defended his doctrine of consent in strictly rational terms; he did not neglect the argument from the natural liberty and equality of man.[34] But, even when considering secular government, he liked to express the doctrine in striking theological imagery. He wrote that, just as Christ was

[31]   G. Kallen (ed.), *De concordantia catholica* in *Nicolai de Cusa opera omnia*, XIV (Hamburg, 1963).
[32]   *De con.*, p. 348.
[33]   p. 205.
[34]   pp. 162, 348.

born of an incorrupt virgin by her free consent, so from the incorrupt congregation of the people true rulership should emerge by free consent[35] — a sort of immaculate conception of the state. In another image, Nicholas called the people a 'divine seedbed' and explained that, since its members had equal natural rights (*naturalia iura*), licit authority could be derived only through their voluntary subjection to a ruler.[36]

Nicholas agreed with the common view that consent could be expressed by the greater part of a community and he was confident that the greater part could generally be trusted. For the church he found a text of Cyprian asserting that the 'greater and better part' of the priests would always remain in the true faith; and likewise, Nicholas supposed, the weightier part of the people would not fall from the right way in considering the welfare of the state.[37] He saw the force of the argument for hierarchy - that the wise should naturally rule the foolish. But he resolved the apparent difficulty by simply affirming that the foolish would voluntarily consent to the laws of the wise - and so through the operation of natural instinct concord would always be maintained.[38] Nicholas was only thirty when he wrote the *Concordantia*. It is a young man's book, filled with a sort of cosmic optimism and an almost Rousseau-ish faith in the righteousness of the community. God was in his heaven; given a little human co-operation all would soon be right with the world.

Nicholas was concerned principally with the right ordering of the church. As for the 'populist' side of his thought here, the foundation of all his ecclesiology was a conviction that jurisdiction inhered permanently, inalienably in the whole ecclesiastical community. According to Nicholas this basic pattern of rule was established from the beginning when Christ conferred jurisdiction on the whole church through Peter as a symbol of the church. 'The power of binding and loosing and infallibility and indeviability inhere in the church itself', he wrote.[39] (Nicholas was perhaps influenced directly by Marsilius of Padua here, but overtly he relied for authority on the old Augustinian texts of the *Decretum*.)

For the actual exercise of power ministers were needed and they were properly created by election and consent. The church was by its very nature a free community since only a willing believer was acceptable to Christ; hence coercive force could derive only from consent; and the 'root' of all authority in prelates was not coercive power but ministerial service. Similarly, new laws acquired their obligatory force from the consent of the community that was to be bound by them.[40]

Even in the institution of Peter by Christ himself the rights of the

[35] p. 326.
[36] p. 348.
[37] pp. 106, 314.
[38] pp. 162, 315-17.
[39] pp. 68-9, 190-1.
[40] pp. 285- 302-3, 137.

community were respected. On this point Nicholas quoted the favorite text of the episcopalists, *Dist.* 21 c.2 of the *Decretum*. 'The other apostles received honor and power with Peter . . . and they wanted him to be their head.' But Nicholas gave a special emphasis to the last words. According to him, Christ did not confirm Peter as head of the church until after the Resurrection, when the apostles had already chosen him to be their leader.[41] (Nicholas took this doctrine, one of central importance for his work, from the canonist Guido de Baysio, who in turn derived it from Johannes de Phintona, a Decretist of the thirteenth century.)[42] The original act of institution by Christ provided a model for the appointment of all subsequent prelates - human election and concurrent divine authorization. Moreover, Christ's manner of instituting Peter implied a particular relationship between Peter and the church. Peter could not be greater than the church since his power was in a sense derived from the church; rather the power of the whole community was greater than that of the Roman pontiff. Nicholas wrote that Peter was greater than individuals but the servant of all. He was greatest 'among the apostles considered distributively, but minister and servant of all considered collectively'.[43] And so the old adage that we have traced from Azo's text on the Roman people takes on yet another form. It is now used to explain the fundamental relationship between Peter and the Twelve upon which the whole constitution of the church was based.

Let us turn to the 'pluralism' in Nicholas's thought. This arose from his acceptance of all the basic arguments of the old episcopalists. Here again, Christ himself established the basic pattern, the fundamental constitutional law of the church. He did not confer authority on Peter alone but on all the apostles; he gave to them all the same powers that Peter received (except the office of headship); and in the existing church all bishops were successors of the apostles. Their jurisdiction was not derived from the pope but from election by their subjects with concurrent divine authorization. The pope could not diminish the jurisdiction of bishops for to do so would disturb the right ordering of the church.[44]

The pope, as head, possessed a universal jurisdiction over the whole church, but the inherent authority of the church was not concentrated in him alone. Others, on regional and local levels, shared in it as of right. The authority of ecclesiastical prelates was ultimately of divine origin, but it was precisely divine law that required the consent of a community

---

[41] pp. 153-4, 284, 303.
[42] There seems to be some confusion about the source of this key doctrine. Nicholas himself (p. 284) wrote that he took it from Guido de Baysio who in turn derived it from Johannes de Deo. But Guido actually attributed the text to a certain Io. de F. or Io. de Fan. The siglum would normally refer to Johannes de Fantutiis, but Kallen points out that this canonist lived after Guido and suggests Johannes de Phintona as a possible source. The original text is actually in Johannes de Phintona's *Lectura ad Dist.* 50 c.53, MS Reims, Bibliothèque de la ville 686, fol. 40rb.
[43] *De con.*, pp. 191, 302.
[44] pp. 149-56.

as a condition of licit government. Hence, in considering the structure of church offices, Nicholas envisaged an authority implanted in the community by God and distributed from the community to its representatives at all levels of the hierarchy. The canonists had known two kinds of representation - the virtual symbolizing of a community in its head, and actual delegation of authority by the members; Nicholas suggested that each kind was necessary to the other. A bishop who 'figured' or symbolized his church as a public person had to be appointed 'by election and consent'. The pope, who 'figured' the whole church, was elected by the cardinals and they were often said to represent the universal church in their role as electors; but Nicholas held that for the representation to be effective their authority ought to be actually delegated by the local churches. Indeed, he called this 'the first root of reform'. In a properly constituted church, Nicholas thought, bishops would be elected by the local clergy with concurrent assent of the laity, metropolitans by their bishops with assent of the clergy, cardinals by metropolitans with assent of the bishops, and, finally, the cardinals would elect the pope with the assent of the metropolitans. (Here reality supervened and Nicholas added that if this involved too long a delay the cardinals could elect alone.)[45]

For Nicholas the church was one great community made up of a host of lesser corporate associations. He wrote that, just as the universal church was a mystical body united to Christ, so too each local church was a mystical body united with its prelate.[46] At every level of the hierarchy government was to be conducted in a collegial fashion, especially in the making of new laws - a bishop was to legislate with a diocesan synod, a metropolitan with a provincial synod, a pope with the college of cardinals or a general council. (Laws enacted in this fashion, Nicholas wrote, carried in themselves 'acceptance and confirmation'.)[47] Nicholas saw the whole church as a 'hierarchy of corporations'; his vision of church order could also be described as a kind of ecclesiastical federalism. The early episcopalists had been interested only in the autonomy of each bishop in his own diocese; Nicholas was interested also in their mode of association at all levels. A group of churches could come together through their representatives in a provincial synod, a group of provinces could come together in a national synod, and all the provinces in a general council.[48]

In his theory of the general council Nicholas brought together various earlier elements of thought and developed them in his own characteristic

[45] pp. 200-3.
[46] p. 57.
[47] pp. 136-44. Nicholas repeated the argument of some Roman lawyers that a community could consent to legislation or withhold consent by actual usage or non-usage. But he also held (here developing a canonistic line of thought) that they could consent in the actual process of enactment through participation in a representative council.
[48] P. Sigmund, *Nicholas of Cusa and Medieval Political Thought* (Cambridge, Mass., 1963), pp. 112, 154-7. Sigmund actually used the phrase 'hierarchy of corporations' in discussing Zabarella; it applies equally well to Cusanus.

fashion. Ideally, he held, pope and council legislated together in harmony, and the pope himself was bound by such legislation. (Here Nicholas recalled the old canonistic doctrine on 'state of the church'.)[49] But if disagreement arose then the judgment of the council was preferred to that of the pope. In a case of manifest papal heresy a pope simply fell from his pastoral office and all Christians were to withdraw obedience from him; but where other offenses were involved the members of a council had to judge the pope and if necessary condemn him. A pope was given authority for the 'edification' of the church and could not use it for 'destruction'; if he did so he broke the 'tacit condition' implied at his election, and the council could depose him accordingly. In the last resort, wrote Nicholas, 'the universal council is simply above the pope'. For scriptural authority he appealed to Matthew 18. 17, where Christ said, 'Go tell it to the church', and 'If he will not hear the church let him be to you as a publican and a sinner.' But Nicholas also argued explicitly from his personal theory of representation. The pope symbolized the universal church only 'confusedly'; the assembled members of a council represented it more perfectly because they brought a more immediate delegation of authority from the member churches. Hence the council prevailed over the pope.[50] For Nicholas, we must recall, Peter was greatest among individuals but 'minister and servant of all considered collectively'.

Nicholas devoted the last third of his book to a study of secular government as exemplified in the medieval Empire. Some details of organization were different and the emphasis was different, since Nicholas was mainly concerned with excessive centralization in the church but with centrifugal tendencies in the Empire. However, the underlying principles were the same in the ecclesiastical and secular spheres. Since all power came from God, all rulership had something of the divine about it; but still the emperor's rightful authority came from the voluntary subjection and consent of his subjects. A ruler so constituted became a public person, bearing the will of all, 'the father of individuals . . . the creature of all collectively'. The people were to participate in legislation because 'What touches all ought to be approved by all.'[51] Nicholas himself frequently drew parallels with church government. The imperial electors chose the emperor just as the cardinals chose the pope; their authority was derived from the people as the cardinals' was from the church. The emperor stood to the princes as the pope stood to the bishops of his patriarchate; he was to have a standing council of advisers as the pope had the cardinals; he ought to summon general councils to legislate for the whole realm.[52]

There is a certain progression in the ideas we have considered so far.

[49] *De con.*, p. 209. See above, pp. 16-17.
[50] pp. 178, 183-7, 194-9. The *condicio tacita* is mentioned at p. 198.
[51] pp. 354, 348, 318.
[52] pp. 352, 327-8, 375-6.

The Roman lawyers were concerned with popular consent and with civil rule. The episcopalists were interested in pluralism and in the divine origin of the church's fundamental constitution. Nicholas of Cues drew together all these strands of thought. He was interested primarily in ecclesiology but also in secular government, and he emphasized equally popular consent, pluralistic structures, and divine authorization as characteristics of a rightly ordered community.

Althusius, the last thinker we shall consider here, was concerned primarily with civil government and he claimed to treat it in a purely rational fashion; his discussion of ecclesiology has only a subordinate place in a treatise devoted ostensibly to pure political theory. Moreover, Althusius was not a medieval Catholic but a seventeenth-century German Calvinist. His work, *Politica methodice digesta*, first published in 1603, takes us into a new realm of religious thought and experience. Some scholars have held that it also introduces us to a new way of reflecting on the problems of constitutional government.

ALTHUSIUS

Althusius presented his arguments with a wealth of supporting references to contemporary jurists and theologians, both Protestant and Catholic. At the time when he wrote, the circumstances of the Reformation had already produced a substantial new literature on problems of political theory. Jesuits like Mariana had restated the grounds for resistance to tyranny. Protestant authors had presented a kind of secular analogue for the medieval doctrine on rights of inferior prelates in the church;[53] they wrote of inferior magistrates in the state who likewise derived their authority, not from the monarch, but from 'God through the people'. (Meanwhile the medieval disputes about the structure of the Catholic church itself were flaring up again in the controversies over Gallicanism at the University of Paris.) Althusius of course was familiar with such current ideas. He also knew many medieval authors at first hand including Thomas Aquinas and Marsilius of Padua, whose words he sometimes echoed. Other medieval doctrines were known to him through their transmission by later authors. The *Vindiciae contra tyrannos* for instance, which Althusius often quoted, helped to remind Protestant political theorists of medieval conciliar ideas. But it would be an endless task to trace every 'influence' on Althusius. He was himself a doctor of civil and ecclesiastical law, and it is evident from the great range of his citations that he

---

[53] Melanchthon was perhaps the first to introduce into Protestant thought the idea of inferior magistrates whose authority was derived from the community. He gave as examples 'the bishops', 'the Imperial electors', and 'certain princes in France'. (See Quentin Skinner, *Foundations of Modern Political Thought*, II, 231.) For inferior magistrates in Roman law theory see Myron P. Gilmore, *Argument from Roman Law in Political Thought, 1200-1600* (Cambridge, Mass., 1941).

had access to all the elements of the tradition we have surveyed so far. The problem is to define his position in relation to that tradition.

Ever since Gierke wrote on his work a hundred years ago, Althusius has been regarded as one of the great seminal figures of modern political theory; but there is surprisingly little agreement about him. He is usually regarded as a prototypical federalist, though even this has been disputed. Some see in his work a tendency to state absolutism; others maintain that he dissolved the very substance of the state in a network of private corporations. (But here he was simply pointing out, as lawyers had been doing ever since the twelfth century, that private corporation law could be applied analogically to define a public law for the state.) Most importantly for us, some see Althusius as a typical Calvinist Christian thinker; others assert that his work is of pivotal significance in the development of modern political thought precisely because he created a purely rational theory of the state independent of any specific theological premises, appealing to God only as a remote first cause.

Althusius apparently intended to do this. He complained in the introduction to his work of lawyers who introduced purely juridical material into treatises on politics, and of theologians who 'sprinkled teachings on Christian piety and charity throughout'. It is disconcerting therefore to open Althusius's own work and find endless legal and scriptural quotations scattered over almost every page. This situation is explained perhaps by the full title of Althusius's book, *Politics Methodically Set Forth Illustrated With Sacred and Profane Examples*. Althusius conceded that a political theorist had to borrow from theologians the teachings of the Ten Commandments, for, he held, they were essential to the life of any state. But, apart from that, he apparently intended to construct a pure science of politics and merely to illustrate it with examples drawn from other disciplines. We shall have to consider how far he succeeded in this task.

On the remote origins of society and the state he offered arguments that were rational but quite unoriginal. Like various medieval authors he combined Aristotelian naturalism with Stoic conventionalism and with elements of Christian doctrine. For Althusius, man was by nature a social animal. Also a certain order of rule and subordination existed in all creatures. Althusius considered the hierarchies of nature once again — we even encounter the king of the bees. Like Nicholas of Cues he was inclined to think that inferiors were innately disposed to obey superiors. (Perhaps even more optimistically than Nicholas, he suggested that women are naturally disposed to obey men.) From this natural disposition of rulers and subjects an 'almost divine concord' arose; but all these considerations did not exclude the need for actual voluntary acts to bring men together in civic associations and to constitute governments. In spite of the differences in personal qualities, men were intrinsically equal by natural law; hence rightful jurisdiction could arise only from their voluntary submission and consent. 'Consent is the efficient cause of political association', Althusius affirmed.[54]

A Christian author could not leave God wholly out of the story, but for Althusius God normally worked through the community. 'God assigned to the political community . . . this . . . power of electing.' And even when God personally intervened in the political process he did so through the people. Nicholas of Cues, we saw, held that, in the New Testament, Christ appointed Peter as head of the church but only after the apostles had assented to his leadership; Althusius argued that, in the Old Testament, when God appointed kings, 'the matter was so handled that they were considered to be chosen by the people as well'. But such cases of direct divine intervention were very rare. Althusius held that, normally, peoples are 'divinely instructed by the light of nature' to institute rulers. Once elected, such rulers 'bear and represent the person of the entire realm . . . and of God' (since all power is ultimately from God).[55]

Althusius seems to go beyond the notion of God as a remote first cause in his insistence that the Ten Commandments provide a necessary foundation for all ordered political society. They impose on us duties toward our neighbor that the neighbor can claim as rights. Without them, Althusius wrote, there could be only 'a beastly, stupid, and inhuman life'. Althusius, however, like many earlier writers, regarded the precepts of the Decalogue as universal principles of natural law. He quoted St Paul on this: 'the Gentiles who have not the law do by nature the things contained in the law'.[56]

So far there is nothing in Althusius that will seem unfamiliar to a student of late medieval political theory. Let us turn to the specific structure of constitutional thought that Althusius built on these foundations. I will try to group some of his ideas in the categories we have been using throughout; populism, which we can now without anachronism call popular sovereignty; and pluralism, which we can now without anachronism call federalism.

As to the first, Althusius defined sovereignty as 'a supreme right of universal jurisdiction' and maintained that this right inhered always, inalienably, in a whole people, considered not as a collection of separate individuals but as a corporate whole.[57] Althusius constructed this doctrine in conscious opposition to Bodin's theory of monarchical sovereignty. 'Bodin clamours that these rights of sovereignty cannot be attrib-

54 *Politica* (ed. Friedrich), pp. 15-19, 163 (see n. 3 above). F. S. Carney provides a brief introduction to modern work on Althusius and a partial translation of the text in *The Politics of Johannes Althusius* (Boston, 1964).
55 *Politica*, pp. 139, 177. A similar argument about the appointment of Saul as king was presented in the fourteenth century by Durand of St Pourçain, *De iurisdictione ecclesiastica* (Paris, 1506), fol. 2rb. See above, p. 41.
56 *Politica*, pp. 7, 95, 199.
57 p. 91. Althusius quoted the Roman law of corporations here (*Dig.* 3.4.7.1).

uted to the realm or people . . . I maintain the exact opposite.' Bodin wrote once (incautiously perhaps) of a sovereignty inherent in the whole realm that was transferred to the king. But, Althusius objected, this was to set up a two-fold sovereignty, a sovereignty of the realm and a sovereignty of the ruler; then (arguing rather like the anonymous conciliar spokesman at Constance) he insisted that such an arrangement was impossible. One power had to be greater than the other: and the power of the whole commonwealth, which instituted the king and could depose him, had to be greater than the power of the king. A people did not alienate its own power in instituting a government; ruling officials were 'servants and ministers' of the people. Curiously adapting the old canonistic phrase, Althusius wrote that rulers were 'not called to a plenitude of power but to a share of the solicitude'.[58]

Althusius explained how the sovereignty of the people could coexist with an effective authority of the ruler by the same legal argument that we have been tracing since the time of Azo. The ruler was 'supreme in relation to individuals . . . not in relation to the subjects taken collectively'. The royalist writer, Barclay, had declared that every people sets a king *over* itself. Althusius replied simply, 'Individuals are under the king, all collectively are above him.' Barclay also argued that ecclesiastical rulers were sovereign over the communities that elected them. Althusius maintained the opposite. A pope, bishop, or abbot was subordinate to the electing college of cardinals, church, or monks, since in the last resort the prelate could be deposed for heresy or gross abuse of power. The rights inherent in the college lived on indefinitely; those of the ruler were merely derivative and transitory. Althusius added that the offices of kings were 'not unlike those of ecclesiastical overseers'.[59]

The pluralism in Althusius lies in his insistence that large-scale sovereign states might contain within themselves smaller political units which retained their own autonomous governments based on local consent. Indeed he maintained that the local units were anterior to the sovereign state as cause precedes effect. According to Althusius men first came together, in private associations - families and guilds. The family was a natural association, the guild a civil or voluntary one. A community achieved a political form of association when many families and guilds came together to form a city-state by adopting a common law. Without such a law they were just a crowd; with it they became a *universitas*, a corporate whole. Althusius applied the standard rules of Roman corporation law in elaborate detail to this first political association, and the fact is significant since he described the city as a 'microcosm of the whole realm'. The city retained its identity though the individuals changed. It could be called a *persona ficta*. The ruler, appointed by common consent, was described as a syndic or procurator like the agent of a corporation;

[58] *Politica*, pp. 5, 91-3.
[59] pp. 159, 152-3.

he was greater than individuals but not greater than all collectively. He was assisted by senators representing the community, and ruler and senators again formed a corporate body. Decisions of the senate could be arrived at by a majority vote provided that two-thirds of the members were present; and such decisions were binding on the ruler.[60]

With minor changes these same rules applied also to the higher levels of organization. A cluster of cities formed a province, and a cluster of provinces a *regnum*, a sovereign state, the highest form of political association presided over by an elected king or 'supreme magistrate'. One could well describe Althusius's state in the modern phrase we applied to Nicholas of Cues's church, 'a hierarchy of corporations'. The realm itself, its representative assembly, and the constituent political units within the realm were all conceived of as corporate entities, responsive to the rules of the corporation law. Althusius was more explicitly federalist than his predecessors, though, in specifying with care the ways in which local communities could be associated together in larger political entities. A 'complete confederation' was attained, he wrote, only when the communities shared a common sovereignty on terms defined by a fundamental law. Then they became 'united into one and the same body'. A 'partial confederation' arose when communities bound themselves together by treaties but retained individual rights of sovereignty.[61]

At every level of government - city, province, realm — the form of government was collegial. The ruler of a city had his senate, the provincial governor a provincial assembly of estates, and the king a 'general ecumenical council' or estates-general. Althusius always envisaged a ruler as surrounded by a representative assembly whose consent was required for new legislation and other major acts of government; he wrote that a king or 'supreme magistrate' was required to consult the general council of his realm in all 'difficult, grave and arduous affairs'. (Althusius remembered to quote here the old tag, *Quod omnes tangit*, in a slightly revised form. 'It is just that what touches all should be acted upon by all.') The estates functioned as corporate bodies, reaching decisions by majority votes, and their opinions prevailed over those of the ruler; otherwise, wrote Althusius, there would be no point in having them.[62]

In this new Protestant world the civil ruler also presided over a general council of the church of his realm; but again a decision of the council was binding on the ruler.[63] (To prove this Althusius cited Matthew 18. 17: 'Go tell it to the church.') In general, the organization of the church paralleled that of the state. Jurisdiction inhered in the whole ecclesiastical community; and government was built up, by common consent, from local units through intermediate ones to the general assembly.

[60] pp. 38-47.
[61] p. 128.
[62] pp. 133-4, 321-3.
[63] p. 325.

Althusius finally emphasized the role of the officials he called 'ephors', or 'optimates', a group like the prince-electors of the German empire (or like the cardinals in some medieval theories of church government). They formed an electoral college and permanent council of state for the realm, and they held authority as representatives of the whole people. One of their principal duties was to resist tyranny. Althusius wrote that every compact instituting a king included a 'tacit condition' that the king not use his power to injure the people. If a king violated the fundamental law of the realm, or otherwise broke the compact, he lost his royal power *ipso iure* and became a private person. An individual ephor could resist a tyrant but the formal judgment that he had fallen from office belonged to them all as a collegiate body. Individually each ephor was inferior to the king; collectively they were superior to him. Althusius explained that, just as a general council was above a pope, so too the realm, which the ephors represented, was above the king.[64]

Althusius never referred to Nicholas of Cues. The two men lived in very different worlds; they had different philosophical presuppositions; they used different rhetorics. Yet the patterns of constitutional structure described in their works have evident similarities. At many points Althusius's state seems like a mirror image of Nicholas's church. A cluster of communities forms a universal association; authority resides inalienably in the whole people; legitimate government at every level is based on consent; in case of conflict the assembled representatives of the community prevail over its head. Both authors were jurists and both used juridical materials extensively. Yet neither work was simply a treatise on constitutional law; one was overtly a system of religious thought, the other claimed to be a work of pure political philosophy. We are left then with the question whether Althusius really did make a major innovation in political theory by constructing his whole system through pure political reasoning, independently of the earlier juridical and theological authorities that he knew so well, using them merely as illustrations.

This position seems to me hard to sustain. One can illustrate the difficulty by taking a simple, almost trivial, example - the requirement of two-thirds attendance at a city senate and the validity of decisions taken by a majority of the two-thirds. This arrangement corresponds precisely to the law of corporations in the *Digest*. Althusius does not arrive at it by any reasoning process. The figure of two-thirds is quite arbitrary; one might as well write three-fifths or three-quarters. Roman law does not here illustrate a piece of political reasoning; rather it provides the sole ground for the position adopted. More seriously, the same argument applies to the doctrine, 'The ruler is greater than individuals, less than all collectively', which runs like a recurrent thread through the whole tapestry of Althusius's work. This again is not a proposition of pure reason.

[64] pp. 143-8, 383-4.

Many reasonable people in the seventeenth century denied it.[65] The doctrine is rather derived from a specific Roman law tradition that had been adapted in a particular way by late medieval ecclesiology. Althusius wrote at times as though Roman law was a kind of written reason; in fact it is the heritage of a particular time and place. The same argument applies with even greater force to Althusius's use of Scripture. We have seen how he coolly appropriated the Ten Commandments from the theologians on the assumption that, in defining man's duties to God and his neighbor, they stated universal natural principles essential to the cohesion of all societies. But this is not a self-evident proposition. Not all sophisticated political societies have been based on monotheism or on Old Testament standards of morality. In any case, Althusius went far beyond the Decalogue in expounding the moral precepts that he wove into his theory of the state. In one crucial passage near the beginning of his work, where he was discussing the origin of political society, Althusius cited a dozen passages of St Paul to illustrate the principle that each man should seek his neighbor's good even before his own; then he quoted Cicero, 'We have not been born for ourselves alone, but our country claims a share in us and our friends'; then he mentioned the Old Testament, the Ten Commandments again; and then the Sermon on the Mount, 'You shall love your neighbor as yourself'; and the *Digest* of Justinian, 'injure no one; render to each his due'; and St Paul once more, this time on the variety of spiritual gifts among the members who make up the one body of Christ. All this moved Althusius to further reflection on the divine plan for mankind. God willed that we should all need one another, he wrote, that friendship should bind us all together, that no one should consider another valueless. And it was this chain of thought that led up to the conclusion on which all the subsequent work is founded: 'The efficient cause of political association is consent.[66] It is a rather beautiful concatenation of texts, but it is hardly pure political science.

Althusius no doubt thought that he was founding his system on universal truths of morality that were self-evident or rationally demonstrable. Political theorists had been making this assumption ever since the thirteenth century and would continue to do so down to the eighteenth. But the universal truths of the theorists were really the heritage of a particular religious culture. The essential content of their argument was determined by an ancient Christian or Stoic-Christian view of man and society, which gave rise to radically new constitutional theories when it was applied to the realities of medieval and early modern government. As for Althusius, his work (like that of Cusanus) seems to me unintelligible unless it is seen as the endproduct of a tradition - a particular way

---

[65] For instance, a moderate constitutionalist like Philip Hunton as well as an absolutist like Hobbes.

[66] *Politica*, p. 18.

of interweaving Christian religious and classical legal thought - that can be traced back as far as the twelfth-century Roman and canon lawyers. It would be pleasing if we could trace the tradition forward from Althusius to the American Federalists as Carl Friedrich suggested. There was in fact a stream of German federalist thought that flowed from Althusius through Hugo to Nettelbladt, who was writing at the time of the American Revolution. Rufus Davis has observed that, if constitutional 'alchemy' were possible, the American constitution or something very like it could have been compounded out of elements of German thought. But the Americans never seem to have appealed to these works. I suppose the reason was the actual moribund state of the German Empire at the end of the eighteenth century. As Madison wrote, it was 'a nerveless body incapable of regulating its own members, insecure against external dangers, and agitated with unceasing fermentation in its own bowels'. That was the last place the founding fathers wanted to look in order to find a model for their brave new constitution. Americans had to reinvent federalism for themselves, guided by their own special needs and experiences; but they were working within the same tradition of thought as Althusius, a tradition probably transmitted in their case mainly through other sources of Calvinist political theology.

There are many odd resonances. James Wilson, the Pennsylvania Federalist whom I quoted at the outset, seems to echo Althusius when he writes, 'In all governments . . . there must be a power established . . . which is called supreme. The only question is where that power is lodged. . . . In truth it remains and flourishes with the people. . . . They have not parted with it . . . They can delegate it . . . to such bodies, on such terms, and under such limitations as they think proper.'[67] Or again when Wilson declares, 'The term corporation . . . in its enlarged sense will comprehend the government of Pennsylvania. The existing union of states and even this projected system is nothing more than a formal act of incorporation.'[68] Carl Friedrich was happier with a second metaphor about Althusius and the Federalists. 'We are here not talking of influences necessarily, but of two flowers stemming from the same root.'

There is one last point to be made. The anti-Federalists had a strong case. The systems of thought that I have been describing offer severe difficulties in theory and practice. In principle it is very hard to explain how authority can inhere simultaneously in a ruler and a community or how a bishop and pope can rule simultaneously in the same diocese. Again, it may be licit to argue that a community is always greater than its representative. But it does not follow from this that the assembled representatives of particular provinces are greater than the monarchical head who represents the whole community. Yet conciliarist and Calvinist

[67] Wood, *Creation of the American Republic,* p. 530.
[68] 'Address to a Meeting of the Citizens of Pennsylvania, October 6, 1787', in B. F. Wright, *A Source Book of American Political Theory* (New York, 1929), pp. 259-63 (p. 261).

thinkers often took this for granted. In real life no pope or king was willing to play the role of a mere republican magistrate. A Renaissance pope would not cavil at the title 'servant of the servants of God'; there was a sort of humble magnificence about it; but he would never agree to serve as a subordinate official of a general council. Nor was a king a mere agent of his Estates or parliament. And moderate constitutional thinkers did not want him to be so. They wanted a rule of pope-in-council, king-in-parliament, a system where a monarch ruled with counsel and consent but had still his own monarchical role to play. They were interested primarily in a diffusion of authority within the central government. To explain this pattern of thought and practice they had to turn to a different kind of corporation doctrine, to new ways of adapting the ancient theory of a mixed constitution, and to a more complex analysis of the relationship between ruler and community.

V

Corporate rulership and mixed constitution

We have seen that difficulties could arise in the various systems of ecclesiology and political theory built around the Roman law doctrine, 'The ruler is greater than individuals but not greater than the whole people.' Developed in one way the formula could lead on to an awkward theory of 'double sovereignty' in which both ruler and people had the right to make law. In its more typical forms the doctrine tended to a simple republicanism even if, by courtesy, the supreme magistrate was styled 'emperor' or 'king' or even 'pope'. That is to say, the assembled representatives of the people or a majority of them always prevailed over the ruler who, in the last resort, was conceived of merely as their proctor or agent. And this did not correspond to the facts of life in church or state in most parts of Europe. Moreover, although the constitutional theorists we have considered so far often worried about possible tyranny in a king or pope, it never seems to have occurred to them that a representative assembly might also abuse its powers.

An alternative theory of government grew up in the seventeenth century, influenced in part by English political experience and especially by the crisis of the Civil War, when many people came to realize for the first time that a parliament could be just as oppressive as a king. In this alternative theory tyranny was avoided by a diffusion of authority within a complex central government. The government was composed of several members - in England, king, lords, and commons, in later versions various institutionalized forms of executive, judiciary, and legislative power. No one part of government represented 'the people' against the others; all of them together, considered as a corporate whole, derived their authority from a constitution based on popular consent. No one member could licitly usurp the authority of the others; if dissension arose between the parts of government, no superior institution existed to judge between them. Hence, irreconcilable conflict led to a breakdown of government and a reversion of authority to the people. But the underlying right of the people was not conceived of as a simple right to rule. It was something latent, not a power to govern but a power to establish government - and to re-establish it in case of breakdown - a constitutive power.

These are the ideas whose sources we shall explore next. They were formulated classically by John Locke, but Locke, it seems, derived them in considerable part from George Lawson, an English clergyman of Presbyterian leanings, who wrote a generation earlier in Cromwell's England.[1] (His *Politia sacra et civilis* was completed in 1657.) Lawson is the last major thinker we shall consider. The few modern scholars who have dealt with his work have been concerned to show how all the twists and turns of his thought can be related to the actual circumstances of the 1650s. (It is pointed out, for instance, that Lawson would not acknowledge the legitimacy of Cromwell's usurped power; but he did not recognize the claim of Charles II either; hence he had to argue that a right to constitute a new form of government inhered in the people.) But Lawson's work can also be understood in another way, as a link in a tradition of ecclesiology and political theory that was already centuries old at the time when he wrote; and it is this second way of understanding that we shall try to explore.

Such a roundabout approach to a work that was obviously inspired by the urgent problems of the author's own day may call for a word of explanation. Intellectual historians (I mean scholars in the field of intellectual history) often tell us nowadays that to understand a complex work like Lawson's we must study, not only the text itself (although the structure of Lawson's text is particularly interesting), but also the context in which the work was written. However, one should really write 'contexts' in the plural, for there are many possible ones (the context of family upbringing, of social class, of economic interests, of personal friendships, of region and nation . . .). But two contexts at least must always be taken into account when we consider any sophisticated work of political theory - the actual world of experience which the author was trying to explain, and the inherited world of ideas which helped to shape his attitudes to that experience. Modern work on Lawson has emphasized the first context; hence we can most usefully explore the second one. Moreover a glance at the very varied and cosmopolitan origins of the ideas that were eventually drawn into English seventeenth-century thought may help us avoid what J. H. M. Salmon has called the 'Liberal distortion' of history (a successor to the old 'whig interpretation'), the view that modern constitutional thought is uniquely an expression of 'the English genius' of the seventeenth century. The two ways of investigation - by reference to the immediate political, social, and economic context or by reference to the history of ideas - should not be regarded as rival methodologies. They are really complementary; each needs the other. Historians of constitutional thought might do well to adapt for their own mundane studies the words of the old pagan Symmachus on a higher theme: 'Not by one path alone can men approach so great a mystery.'

[1] A. H. Maclean, 'George Lawson and John Locke', *Cambridge Historical Journal*, 9 (1947), 68-87. See most recently J. H. Franklin, *John Locke and the Theory of Sovereignty* (Cambridge, 1978).

To understand more fully how the seventeenth-century 'world of ideas' came to exist we shall need to trace two further theories of government from the thirteenth century onward, a distinctively medieval theory of corporate rulership and a revived, ancient theory of mixed government, for these two doctrines became fused in various seventeenth-century attempts to explain the structure of parliament and the interrelationship of its various members. We shall also have to consider the development of more sophisticated ideas concerning the relationship of government to community. And finally we shall need to advert to the distinction, raised in the first lecture, between a simple Roman law theory of corporations and a complex canon law theory.

These may seem esoteric notions to apply to the simple-minded country gentry in the House of Commons whose real motivations, we well know, were economic self-interest, passionate hatred of Charles's supposed popery and tyranny, and reluctant loyalty to their duly crowned and consecrated king. But not all the gentry were simple-minded. Some of them were scholars and many of them were lawyers. The vocabularies of mixed constitution and of corporation law were in fact frequently deployed in the pamphlet warfare of the 1640s. Charles himself, seeking a last-minute accommodation with parliament, formally declared in 1642 that England was ruled by a mixed government of monarchy, aristocracy, and democracy - king, lords, and commons. His declaration was widely taken to mean that sovereignty inhered in a corporate association of the king and the two houses. William Prynne wrote, 'King, Lords, and Commons by the Common Law make but one intire Corporation', and he went on to argue that in this corporative association, although the king was greater than each individual, he was less than the two houses, since they represented the whole people. They were superior, he wrote, 'as a General Council is above the Pope, the Chapter above the Bishop, the University above the Chancellor'.[2] Prynne cited respectable sources here, but the argument is not without difficulties. The relationship between pope and council was disputed at this time; a chapter was not greater than its bishop; and to confuse a chapter and a bishop with a university and its chancellor was simply to confuse two different theories of corporation structure.

CORPORATIONS: SIMPLE AND COMPLEX

Let me remind you briefly of those theories. In the simple model all power resided in the community and its exercise was delegated to a presiding officer who was essentially a subordinate agent of the community. This theory, which Prynne was implicitly applying to king and parliament, bears little resemblance to any traditional doctrine of English monarchy. The canonistic or complex theory of corporation structure offers

[2]   *The Soveraigne Power of Parliaments and Kingdoms* (London, 1643), I, 41; IV, 153.

Having provided this rather flimsy scriptural justification, Hostiensis turned, perhaps with a sigh of relief, to the Roman and canon law, where he was truly a master, for the rest of his arguments. He cited the Roman law on the ancient senate to prove that the cardinals were 'parts of the body of the lord pope'. But above all he relied on the canon law of corporations. 'The union between the pope and the college of the Roman church is much greater and more excellent even than that between any other patriarch and his chapter', he wrote, 'and yet a patriarch ought not to settle difficult matters without the counsel of his brothers.' Then Hostiensis gave references to other parts of his work where he had discussed in elaborate detail the mutual obligations subsisting between prelates and chapters.

In all this there was no argument that the pope was merely the equal of a cardinal, any more than a bishop was merely the equal of a cathedral canon. The pope was pre-eminent. He was head of the college of the Roman church, the cardinals members. But ruling authority resided in the whole corporate body. Quite consistently, Hostiensis maintained that, in a papal vacancy, the cardinals succeeded to the papal jurisdiction and that they could exercise it at least if there were great need. He brushed aside the argument that the cardinals would be a body without a head. Christ himself was always their head, he declared. (The view that Christ's invisible headship maintained the unity of the church during a papal vacancy was often expressed later during the Great Schism and it perhaps helped to prepare the way for the Protestant view that no earthly head was needed at all.) Hostiensis also held that, if the whole college became extinct during a papal vacancy, its authority devolved to the Roman people. They could then either reinstitute a government for the church or summon a general council to do so.[10]

Hostiensis's doctrine was later drawn into more complex theories in which pope, cardinals, and council together were conceived of as a corporate ruling entity. In the fifteenth century, for instance, Peter d'Ailly claimed a major role for the cardinals within a general council, appealing for authority to both Hostiensis and Laurentius (whose work he knew through Guido de Baysio).[11] Hostiensis himself never considered the situation that would arise if the whole college of cardinals fell into conflict with a reigning pope; but when Cardinal Zabarella took up these questions at the time of the Great Schism he maintained that the cardinals could withdraw from the pope and appeal to the universal church.[12] However this is getting ahead of our story. Let us just note for the moment that Hostiensis had already formulated as ecclesiology the doctrine of corporate rulership that Christopher Besold would state centu-

10   *Com. ad* X.5.38.14, 1.6.6.
11   For d'Ailly the corporate Roman church, composed of pope and cardinals, was the 'principal part' or 'principal member' of a general council. See his *De ecclesiae . . . autoritate* in Gerson, *Opera omnia* (ed. E. du Pin), II (Antwerp, 1706), col. 938.
12   *Tractatus de schismate,* in Schardius, pp. 698-702.

---

a more promising model. In this theory a prelate was regarded as the head of the corporate body over which he presided. He entered upon an established office with its own inherent powers and dignity; he acquired a unique status as a virtual representative, a personification, of his church; but still he was required to rule with counsel and consent of the members in grave matters. (King Henry VIII presumably had some such form of association in mind when he said, 'We be informed by our judges that we at no time stand so highly in our estate royal as in the time of Parliament, wherein we as head and you as members are conjoined and knit together in one body politic.') In a complex corporation, head and members ruled co-ordinately. Normally the participation of both parties was required in major affairs; but exceptionally, if a prelate became incompetent, the chapter could exercise some of his powers; and likewise, if a chapter was grossly negligent, the exercise of its powers could devolve temporarily to the prelate.

Ideas analogous to these were put forward rather commonly in the English constitutional debates of the seventeenth century. The parliamentarian, Charles Herle, for instance, used almost interchangeably the language of mixed government and of corporation law. 'Now as to this mixture [of government]', he wrote, ''tis not personal but incorporate and corporations, the law says, die not.' English government, Herle wrote, was 'a coordinative and mixed monarchy'. He added: '. . . monarchy or highest power, is itself compounded of three coordinate estates'. And he quoted the rule of corporation law, *coordinata invicem supplent,* 'coordinates supplement each other'. In the present case, since the king had failed to fulfill his duty faithfully, his power devolved to the two houses.[3] When civil war broke out the parliamentary leaders denied that they were fighting against the king. They claimed to be fighting for the corporate whole of king-and-parliament against the erring person of Charles. On the royalist side, John Bramhall held that the king himself was the 'principal member' of parliament and that, in case of conflict, the king was to be obeyed as virtually representing the whole realm.[4]

There was an underlying incoherence in these theories that only slowly became apparent to their seventeenth-century exponents. Neither the doctrine of mixed government nor the complex model of corporation structure (the only relevant model) permitted one party in government simply to arrogate to itself the rights of another. If, in case of dispute, any one part of a mixed constitution could claim a higher authority than the rest, that part was ultimately sovereign and the principle of mixture was destroyed. (Phillip Hunton pointed this out in 1643.) Likewise, in corporation law, if a bishop and chapter fell into a dispute about their respective rights (and such disputes were very common), neither had a

3   *A Fuller Answer to a Treatise Written by Dr Ferne* (London, 1642), pp. 3, 8, quoted by Franklin, pp. 28-9.
4   *The Serpent-Salve,* in *Works of John Bramhall,* III (Oxford, 1844), 326, 380-1.

valid claim simply to override the other. The matter had to be litigated before a superior judge. But in a conflict between king and parliament no superior judge existed. The same problem could present itself in the church in the case of a conflict between pope and cardinals or, more intransigently, between pope and general council. The existence of the problem was already perceived in the years around 1200 when various canonists began to ask who should be obeyed in a conflict between the pope and 'all the bishops' - and usually gave indecisive answers. The awareness of the problem (and its recurrence in a variety of practical contexts) gave a persistent stimulus to reflection on the internal structure of government and on the relationship between government and community from the thirteenth century onward.

Ernst Kantorowicz, commenting on corporative concepts of government in England, has observed, 'There is hardly a phrase or metaphor ... which could not be traced back to some antecedents in the legal writings of the thirteenth century.'[5] Other historians have traced various antecedents of the theory of English government as a form of mixed constitution. But, to comprehend adequately the difficulties inherent in seventeenth-century constitutional thought, and the ways in which those difficulties were resolved, we need to examine a little more closely the interplay between these two doctrines in earlier centuries - how they originated, how they were adapted in earlier disputes, the overtones of meaning they had acquired.

CORPORATE HEADSHIP

We may note first that there is an immediate source for the conflation of the two doctrines - corporate rulership and mixed constitution - in Christopher Besold, a critic of Bodin, writing about 1600. Bodin had maintained that the idea of a mixed constitution was logically absurd since sovereignty was of its nature indivisible. Besold replied that a mixed government could be composed of a single ruler and a number of subordinates without compromising the principle of indivisibility, provided that sovereignty was attributed to 'the whole ruling college or corporation'. He acknowledged that the single ruler would have to be conceded greater eminence than the rest; otherwise the constitution would be a simple aristocracy. But the individual ruler would not enjoy the full right of sovereignty in himself; rather it would inhere in the corporate body as a whole.[6] Besold's work was known to a few English authors of the Civil War period, including Lawson.

Such complicated ideas did not suddenly appear for the first time in 1600 as a response to Bodin's theory of unitary sovereignty. To understand their origins and early development we must again, as usual, turn

[5] *King's Two Bodies*, p. 401.
[6] *Operis politici* (Strasbourg, 1641), p. 176.

back to the world of medieval ecclesiology, and specifically to some thirteenth-century reflections on the structure of the Roman church, the 'head of all the churches'. The idea that the universal church was ruled, not simply by a monarchical pope, but by a complex corporate sovereign, grew from the actual powers that the cardinals had acquired from the mid eleventh century onward as councillors and electors of the pope. The college of cardinals in its eleventh-century form was really a new institution, but soon 'prefigurings' of it were found in both the Old and New Testaments, and even before 1100 the claim was advanced that 'the privilege of Peter belongs to the whole Roman see, not to the pope alone'.[7]

Around 1200 the principal advocate of the cardinals' claims was the canonist Laurentius, who held that the pope could not establish a general law touching the universal state of the church without their participation. But the first systematic, highly wrought doctrine of the cardinals' collegiate authority was developed a little later by Hostiensis, writing in the 1260s. Hostiensis was reputed to be the greatest canonist of his age; he was also himself a cardinal and he had a high regard for the dignity of the sacred college. In one passage of his great *Commentaria* on the *Decretales*, Hostiensis declared that he wrote to refute those who denied to the cardinals the rights of a corporation, those who maintained that they were merely individuals, 'called from divers parts of the world and appointed to divers churches'. On the contrary, Hostiensis maintained the cardinals were a 'supreme and excellent college, united by God to the pope, one and the same with him', who met together as a college to govern the affairs of the whole world.[8] According to Hostiensis, Christ had conferred plenitude of power (sovereignty one might say) upon the Roman church; but that power did not reside in the pope merely as an individual person; rather it inhered in the corporate body of pope and cardinals. Hostiensis produced a novel and rather audacious piece of scriptural exegesis to justify this position. An earlier decretal of Pope Innocent III had quoted - or slightly mis-quoted - a Pauline phrase, 'Do you not know that you shall judge angels', and had applied it to the pope and to the cardinals as his 'coadjutors'. Commenting on this Decretal, Hostiensis wrote, 'It is not said "Thou shalt judge" in the singular, but "You shall judge" in the plural in order that not only the pope but all the cardinals should be included in the expression of the plenitude of power.'[9]

[7] J. B. Sägmüller, *Die Thätigkeit und Stellung der Kardinäle bis Papst Bonifaz VIII* (Freiburg, 1896), p. 235. See, more recently, G. Alberigo, *Cardinalato e collegialità* (Florence, 1969) and Karl Morrison, *Tradition and Authority in the Western Church, 300–1140* (Princeton, 1969).

[8] Laurentius, Gloss *ad* C.25 q.1 c.6 (*Foundations*, p. 81). Hostiensis, *Com. ad* X.5.6.17. For further discussion see my 'Hostiensis on Collegiality', *Proceedings of the Fourth International Congress of Medieval Canon Law* (Vatican City, 1976), pp. 401–9, and J. A. Watt, 'Hostiensis on *Per venerabilem*: The Role of the College of Cardinals', in B. Tierney and P. Linehan (eds.), *Authority and Power* (Cambridge, 1980), pp. 193–218.

[9] *Com. ad* X.4.17.3.

ries later as political theory. A large-scale society could be ruled by a collegiate head. One man was pre-eminent, but sovereignty inhered, not in him alone, but in the whole corporate body. Besold regarded this as a form of mixed constitution. We next have to consider the medieval development of this second idea.

MIXED CONSTITUTION

The theory of a mixed constitution is ancient, of course, and secular in origin. It is found in Aristotle, Polybius, Cicero, and various other classical authors. In its most characteristic form the theory affirms that, while monarchy, aristocracy, and democracy all have their distinctive vices and virtues, the best, most stable, constitution will be one that somehow combines all three forms of government. This idea recurs in Renaissance thought, especially in Florence and Venice. It was assimilated into English constitutional doctrine and was adopted by Charles I in 1642 as we noted. The idea remained important in eighteenth-century America.

The classical and Renaissance versions of the doctrine have been investigated in some detail by modern historians - most recently by John Pocock in a major work of synthesis.[13] Pocock emphasizes a tradition of thought derived from classical republicanism and developed by the civic humanists of the fifteenth century who were writing at the same time as the conciliarists of Constance and Basle. (Perhaps we shall eventually learn to see civic humanism and conciliarism as two alternative rhetorical strategies through which the communal ethos of the Middle Ages was transmitted to the early modern world.)[14] In the tradition explored by Pocock the mixed constitution was seen as a possible defense against the persistent tendencies to corruption engendered by the vicissitudes of time that threaten the integrity of a state. Fascinating as the argument is, one may observe that there are few areas where Garrett Mattingly's remark is more relevant - that the medieval church seems to 'foreshadow and as it were recapitulate in advance the development of the modern state'.

There is in fact a whole chapter of medieval ecclesiastical thought about the theory of a mixed constitution that has been less explored than the secular tradition and that needs to be explored if we are to understand all the sources of seventeenth-century doctrine. Throughout the period we are considering, the doctrine of mixed government was developed as much in ecclesiology as in political theory and, even in the eighteenth century, it was expressed as often in religious as in secular language. The major change in the formulation of the doctrine that occurred during the

13 John G. H. Pocock, *The Machiavellian Moment* (Princeton, 1975).
14 There are various interconnections between the two movements. Zabarella, the greatest canonist-conciliarist, was also 'Cardinal of Florence' and acquainted with humanist circles there. (Poggio Bracciolini preached his funeral oration.) On the other hand Leonardo Bruni was a canonist by training.

Middle Ages was that, in classical thought, the idea of a mixed constitution was applied only to the small-scale society of the polis, the city-state; in medieval thought it was applied to a whole nation or a whole church. The ecclesiastical theory of a mixed constitution arose in a peculiar way. It grew from a belief that God had established an ideal government for his Chosen People in the Old Testament and that, like a good Aristotelian, God had perceived that a mixed constitution was the best form of rule he could devise. Once enunciated, this idea displayed an extraordinary vitality and, since Israel could be regarded as a prototype of both nation and church, it found a wide range of applications. In seventeenth-century England the idea of an ideal government in ancient Israel became entangled with the Puritan notion of the English as an 'elect nation'. Eighteenth-century Americans too were fond of regarding themselves as a new Israel. When a design for the Great Seal of the United States was being discussed, Jefferson wanted it to show the Chosen People in the wilderness complete with fiery pillar; but Franklin preferred a more dramatic scene of the Red Sea opening up to swallow the chariots of Pharaoh, while Moses looked smugly on. Along with the ancient Israelites Jefferson wanted his seal also to depict Hengist and Horsa, 'the Saxon chiefs from whom we claim the honor of being descended and whose political principles and form of government we have assumed'. It is odd how, in eighteenth-century thought, ancient Jews and ancient Germans jostled one another for the honor of inventing the American constitution. For such imagery had specific constitutional implications. In colonial thought the mixed constitution of Israel was often identified with the mixed or balanced government of England. Until a break with the mother country became inevitable, colonial preachers declaimed happily about the excellent constitution of 'God's British Israel'.[15]

All this later fantasy was derived ultimately from a very sober source, the *Summa Theologiae* of Thomas Aquinas, where, for the first time in medieval thought, the government of Moses was associated with the mixed constitution of Aristotle.[16] We have seen how, in contexts dealing with the origins and legitimacy of government, Thomas appealed often to the doctrine of natural hierarchy and upheld monarchy as the best form of rule. But in other contexts he argued for a widespread popular participation in the actual conduct of government; and the two doctrines came together in his theory of a mixed constitution. In developing his ideas on these questions Thomas provides many examples of the interplay between religious and secular constitutional thought that we have mentioned so often. At one point in the *Summa,* for instance, he discussed St Paul's argument on the different states and offices in the

[15]   On the Great Seal see J. P. Boyd (ed.), *The Papers of Thomas Jefferson,* I (Princeton, 1950), 494-5. For the imagery of 'God's British Israel' see N. O. Hatch, *The Sacred Cause of Liberty* (New Haven, 1977).

[16]   There is a still earlier precedent in the first-century work of Philo, but Philo's teaching did not give rise to a continuing tradition of thought.

church: 'As in one body we have many members but all the members have not the same office, so we being many are one body in Christ' (1 Cor. 12.12). Then at the end of the discussion Thomas applied the Pauline argument specifically to secular government: 'an earthly commonwealth is the better preserved by a distinction of duties and states, since thereby the greater number have a share in public actions. Wherefore the Apostle says that "God hath tempered us together that . . . the members might be mutually careful for one another".'[17]

In another passage, Thomas asked whether an independent people had the right to change existing laws by practicing new customs (the old argument of the jurists now recurring in a theological context). There were various arguments against this right. Human law was based on natural and divine law, and so should not be changed. An individual act against the law was wrong; therefore a multiplicity of such acts, constituting a custom, could not be right. And only rulers could make law, while customs were established by private individuals. Against all this Thomas cited only one authority, but this one text proved quite decisive. 'St Augustine says "The customs of the people of God . . . are to be considered as laws. And those who throw contempt on the customs of the Church ought to be punished".'[18] Here again an argument from ecclesiology is used to settle a point of political theory. Thomas seems to move between the two spheres almost unconsciously.

It is the same with the theory of a mixed constitution. The issue arose when Thomas considered the form of government divinely established for the children of Israel, and raised an apparent objection against God's provision for them. Royal government, Thomas argued, was the most perfect form of rule since monarchy most closely resembled the divine governance of the universe; but God did not establish a king over Israel from the beginning. Therefore, it seemed, he gave an imperfect form of government to his Chosen People. In response Thomas acknowledged that monarchy was the best simple form of regime; but, after quoting Aristotle on the advantages of popular participation in government and on the varieties of licit constitutions, he concluded that a mixed form (including monarchy) was better than any simple one.

Hence the best form of government in any city or kingdom is where one is set in authority on account of his virtue to rule over all; and under him are others ruling on account of their virtue; and nevertheless such government belongs to all, both because the rulers can be chosen from all and because they are chosen by all.

Thomas then argued, by some slightly strained exegesis of Exodus and Deuteronomy, that God had indeed instituted such a regime in the days of Moses and so had provided the most perfect form of government for Israel. Moses ruled over all, so he was a kind of king; but he was assisted by seventy-two elders who formed an aristocracy; also the elders were

[17] *Summa theol.* 2.2ae.183.2.
[18] *Summa theol.* 1.2ae.97.3.

'chosen from all the people' and 'the people chose them' so there was also present an element of democracy. Thomas summed up, 'Such is any well-mixed polity; [it is mixed] from kingship since there is one at the head of all; from aristocracy in so far as a number of persons are set in authority on account of their virtue; from democracy, that is the power of the people, in so far as the rulers can be chosen from the people and the people have a right to choose their rulers.'[19]

Thomas made a distinctive contribution here. He quoted Aristotle and the Bible but the precise doctrine he presented does not really exist in either of his sources. Thomas did not just deck out an Aristotelian idea in Old Testament dress; he adapted the idea in the process of adopting it. Aristotle had indeed mentioned a three-fold form of mixed government in connection with the constitution of Sparta, but all his more detailed discussions dealt only with a mixture of aristocracy and democracy. Aristotle was basically interested in securing a stable balance of class interests in the state; Thomas was more interested in uniting in one government the excellences proper to each simple regime. Monarchy ensured unity, aristocracy wisdom, and democracy liberty. Thomas also introduced a kind of 'checks and balances' approach in his commentary on Aristotle's *Politics*. The mixed regime was best, he wrote, because each element checked, 'tempered', the other two. Again, while many classical authors suggested that there should be a democratic element in the ideal constitution, they did not maintain that the democratic element consisted in a right of the people to choose the monarchic and aristocratic elements. But such an idea does begin to suggest modern constitutional theory where a complex central government derives its authority from the consent of the people. And it is in this form, after passing through a filter of medieval theology, that the idea of a mixed constitution was most influential for the future.

We might call Thomas's theory the Mosaic model of a mixed constitution. Alongside it there grew up another ecclesiastical theory, based on what I might call the 'Peter principle' or 'Peter paradigm', which had equal success. Everyone knows that the theory of papal monarchy was based on Christ's words to Peter in the New Testament; only specialists seem to know that many other theories of church government were based on them too. It depends on which text we choose and how we choose to interpret it. The words 'Thou art Peter and on this rock I will build my church' at Matthew 16.18 could indicate a simple monarchy. But if we look at the following words, 'Whatsoever thou shalt bind on earth . . .', we find that Christ addressed those same words to all the apostles at Matthew 18.18, and this could mean that he established an aristocracy in the apostles and their successors. But again, in the same chapter of Matthew (18.15-17), we find: 'If your brother sin against you . . . go tell it to

---

[19]   *Summa theol.* 1.2ae.105.1. Moses of course was chosen by God but Thomas regarded this as being an exception made because 'that people was ruled under the special care of God'.

the church.' And this could mean that Christ had established a kind of democracy, had conferred jurisdiction primarily on the whole Christian community. All these possibilities were explored in medieval ecclesiology. Eventually the idea occurred to some conciliar thinkers that Christ had meant to establish all three forms of government simultaneously. Once formulated, this idea was endlessly repeated by later writers, both Catholic and Protestant. From many possible examples we might cite John Robinson, the chaplain of the pilgrim fathers on the *Mayflower:* 'Now wise men . . . have approved as good and lawful three kinds of polities; monarchical . . . aristocratical . . . and democratical. And all these three forms have their place in the church of Christ.' (In Protestant theories, of course, Christ himself, rather than the pope, was taken to represent the monarchical element.)

To return to the thirteenth century: so far we have seen two ideas emerging in the years just after 1250, an idea of corporate headship with Hostiensis and an idea of mixed constitution with Aquinas. So far as I have noticed the first work in which the two theories were conflated together was the little treatise of Peter Olivi on the abdication of Pope Celestine V. Writing in 1294, Olivi discussed the role of the cardinals as electors and councillors of the pope. Like Hostiensis, he held that the cardinals shared in the power of the Roman see and he specifically used the corporation image, the analogy with other bishops and chapters, in explaining their position. Then he moved at once to a discussion of the forms of constitution in Aristotle's *Politics* and concluded that, since the cardinals represented the whole Christian people, the various elements of Aristotle's mixed polity were indeed reflected in the government of the church.[20]

Olivi offered only a few passing comments. A few years later John of Paris used both corporation theory and the Mosaic model of a mixed constitution more systematically in discussing the structure of the church. John was the first major political philosopher who appealed overtly to corporation law in arguing that a pope was liable to deposition by the whole church or by the cardinals acting on behalf of the church (though in fact his references to inferior corporations did not precisely prove the point he was trying to make).[21] He also repeated the teaching of Aquinas that God had established a kind of Aristotelian mixed constitution for Israel. But then John went further and praised this model as the best form of government for the church of his own day. 'In a mixed constitution', he wrote, 'all have some share in government . . . everybody loves a government of this type . . . it would certainly be the best

---

[20] *De renuntiatione*, in *Archivum Franciscanum Historicum* 11 (1918), 354-6.

[21] Bleienstein, p. 95; Watt, p. 101. John argued here that, just as a monastic community or cathedral chapter could act to depose a delinquent abbot or bishop, so too the pope could be deposed. But the monks or chapter could 'act' only in the sense of bringing an action before a superior judge. On papal deposition by cardinals or general council see also Bleienstein, pp. 140, 201-2, 206; Watt, pp. 159, 243, 249.

constitution for the church.'[22] Again, considering the whole church as a corporate body with the pope as its head, John of Paris called the pope the 'principal member', the 'supreme member of the universal church'; but he added in another context that 'the pope with a council is greater than a pope alone'.[23]

What is lacking in John's discussions is any precise, specific explanation of the distribution of power among the various parts of his corporate church or mixed constitution. His closest approach to a solution was formulated in highly ambiguous terms. Granting that the pope's power was the highest that inhered in any individual person, he argued that 'there is still an equal to him or even greater in the college of cardinals or in the whole church'.[24] In any theory of mixed government it matters a great deal whether the power outside the monarchical head is 'equal' or 'greater' and whether it inheres in a representative college or in the whole community or in both. A century after John of Paris, the crisis of the Great Schism made such questions matters of urgent debate.

GERSON AND THE GREAT SCHISM

The foundation of all conciliar thought in the age of the Schism was a conviction that the community of the church could not be destroyed by any failure of its head. The old texts on indefectibility and inerrancy were now deployed to prove that in no conceivable emergency could the church lack the means to preserve itself, to establish for itself a united government, to exercise what would later be called a constitutive power. The conciliarists were also determined that the form of government to be constituted should serve to protect the church in the future from the corruptions that, they believed, had grown up in the past from the abuse of absolute papal power.

In discussing the indefectibility of the Christian community, John Gerson wrote that the church, as a mystical body, always maintained its intrinsic unity even in the absence of an earthly head through adhesion to its true 'head and spouse', Christ himself. Nevertheless, Christ willed also a visible unity under a true pope, his vicar on earth. 'The church flees from and abhors its own division', wrote Gerson. He held that inherent in the church was 'an infinite creativeness in preserving itself', an ability to 'give itself life and achieve healthy unity'.[25]

Among the many conciliarist authors, Gerson perhaps wrote most interestingly on all the themes we are presently pursuing - corporate rule

---

[22] Bleienstein, p. 175; Watt, pp. 206-7.
[23] Bleienstein, pp. 91-2, 185; Watt, pp. 97, 219.
[24] Bleienstein, p. 207; Watt, p. 250.
[25] *Propositio facta coram Anglicis*, in P. Glorieux (ed.), *Jean Gerson. Oeuvres complètes* (Paris, 1960-73), VI, 125-35 (pp. 126-7).

and mixed constitution, Moses and Peter and Aristotle as guides to the right ordering of the church. He did not pull all the various threads of thought together very tidily. Gerson was not a systematic constitutional theorist; he was a theologian, and a mystical theologian at that. But he was passionately concerned to end the schism in the church and he eagerly, eclectically seized on every argument that could serve this end. Also his works were widely read for centuries after his death and were quite often quoted by constitutional theorists of the seventeenth century. Hence, although Gerson was not a great systematic thinker in this sphere, he was a very influential transmitter of medieval constitutional thought to early modern writers. We can conveniently illustrate his ideas from the treatise *On Ecclesiastical Power* which Gerson read to the Council of Constance in 1417.

The kind of ecclesiastical power that concerns us is the one Gerson called 'external jurisdiction' - the power to rule, to judge, to legislate. This power, he wrote, inhered primarily in the whole church and it was conferred on the church by Christ in the words of Matthew 18.17, 'Go tell it to the church.' 'Without doubt the whole plenitude of power of the material sword is founded on this text', declared Gerson. But this power existed in the scattered church only latently, only as raw 'matter' in the Aristotelian sense, only potentially.[26] The scattered, diffused church could not exercise its own inherent power. But it could constitute a general council to do so. Normally the power of summoning a council belonged to the pope but, if he refused to act and thus endangered the church, an inherent right to assemble resided with the whole community. It was the same, wrote Gerson, with a chapter and dean 'or any corporation and its rector'.[27] In the fifteenth century one did not have to be a professional jurist to think easily in terms of corporation structure. Experience with corporate bodies was a part of everyday life. Gerson was no canonist but he was chancellor of the University of Paris and had been dean of the collegiate church of St Donatien.

Gerson's thought revolved around two poles - his affirmation of the supreme authority of the whole body of the church and his acknowledgement of the headship of the pope within that body. Up to a point he reconciled the two doctrines quite neatly. The universal church included the papal power; therefore, to ask whether the whole church was greater than the pope was simply to ask whether a whole was greater than a part. Also, the same argument could be applied to a general council. Gerson defined the council as an assembly of 'every hierarchical state of the whole Catholic church, no faithful person who wishes to be heard being excluded'. It followed from the definition that a general council could not exist as such unless it included the power of the papacy (the foremost hierarchical state); and this Gerson consistently maintained.

---

[26] *De potestate ecclesiastica, Oeuvres,* VI, 210-50 (pp. 216, 217).
[27] pp. 222, 233, 240.

Hence he could argue that the whole council, because it included the papal power, was greater than an individual pontiff. To account for the actual situation at the Council of Constance in 1417 (when no generally acknowledged pope existed) Gerson further explained: 'If a general council is to represent the church sufficiently and integrally, it is necessary that it include the papal authority, whether there is a pope or whether he is lacking through natural or civil death.[28] Gerson was arguing, in effect, that the council formed a corporate whole in which the power that belonged to the head devolved to the members during a vacancy, a common doctrine of canonistic corporation law. Gerson even conceded that papal power as such might be superior to the rest of ecclesiastical power; but then, he argued, 'the rest' could not constitute a general council.[29]

Gerson's arguments thus far established quite persuasively the old doctrine that 'a pope with a council is greater than a pope alone'. But, given the actual circumstances of the schism, he had to argue further that the members of a council could exercise authority over the head, even to the point of deposing him if necessary. 'In some cases a pope can be judged by a council', Gerson wrote. But, according to his own previous argument, the council could not act as a council unless it already included the papal power. Gerson tried to solve the problem by expanding an earlier statement. Papal power could be taken away, he wrote, 'by natural death . . . or by civil, namely by deposition'.[30] This argument would have met his difficulty if he had been willing to concede that a pope who fell into heresy or grave crime automatically stripped himself of his own office. (One could then say that papal power had devolved to the council.) But Gerson would not accept this position. Such a view seemed to him to smack of the Wycliffite error that a ruler lost his intrinsic right to rule whenever he fell from divine grace. Gerson held therefore that, just as a pope could acquire office only by formal election, so too he could lose it involuntarily only by formal deposition.[31] But this involved him in a self-contradiction. The council could not exercise its jurisdiction as a council unless it included the papal power; but it could not include the papal power until it had already deposed the existing pope. Gerson never really resolved this tension in his thought. In his more conservative moods he wrote as though the council was a complex corporate entity in which the pope as head possessed his own independent dignity and status; but in his more radical arguments he treated the council as a 'simple' corporation in which the head could readily be deposed by the will of the members.

In the discussions that we have considered so far Gerson was treating the general council as a corporate body representing the church, though

---

[28]   p. 222.
[29]   p. 233.
[30]   p. 223.
[31]   This position was developed most fully in Gerson's *De auferibilitate*, *Oeuvres*, III, pp. 294-313 (pp. 307-9).

he was ambivalent in considering what kind of a corporation it was. He also approached the parallel doctrine of mixed constitution from several points of view. In one discussion he presented the Mosaic constitution as a model for ecclesiastical government and described it as a three-fold polity, 'regal in Moses, aristocratic in the seventy-two elders, and democratic since under Moses rulers were taken from the people and single tribes'.[32] Another argument started out from the New Testament texts about the founding of the church. Gerson held to the usual conciliarist view that Christ conferred jurisdiction not only on Peter but also on the twelve apostles and seventy-two disciples, the prototypes of bishops and priests; but he went beyond this widely held opinion and asserted that every other hierarchical order in the church was established from the beginning 'at least in germ' - papacy, cardinalate, patriarchate, archepiscopate, episcopate, and priesthood. Hence, since a general council included all states and dignities in the church, it necessarily included, at least virtually, 'every political regime, papal, imperial, royal, aristocratic and democratic'.[33]

Finally, at the end of his work, Gerson explicitly quoted Aristotle's *Politics* on the different forms of rule and asserted that the government of the church was indeed a kind of Aristotelian mixed polity. The pope represented monarchy, the cardinals aristocracy, and the council democracy;[34] or rather, wrote Gerson, correcting himself, the council was that perfect polity that resulted from a mixture of all three forms. Once again, a classical, secular constitutional theory had undergone a significant transmutation in being adapted to fit the contours of medieval ecclesiology.

But in this argument there was again a crucial point that Gerson left dangling. It is the same point that arose in his discussions on the deposition of a pope. He found it easy to assert that the power of the papacy could be wielded by a council when no pope existed or no clearly legitimate one. But how would power be shared among the constituent parts of a mixed government when a certainly legitimate pope came to preside over a future general council? The more moderate conciliarists at Constance were always reticent on this point and they often fell back on ambiguous formulas. (Peter d'Ailly observed: 'The pope is greatest in a council but he is not greater than a council.') Gerson usually wrote as though it could simply be taken for granted that the members would prevail over the head; but he never explained how this presumption could be reconciled with the view that papal authority - as the monarchical element - was a necessary constituent part of the mixed government constituted by a general council. One might say of Gerson, as of John of

---

[32] *De pot.*, p. 225.
[33] pp. 222, 240.
[34] p. 248. Gerson used the word timocracy, one of Aristotle's terms for the 'good' form of democracy.

Paris, that he did not explain adequately the distribution of power in his mixed constitution.

During the Council of Basle the issue grew clearer. When pope and council fell into irreconcilable conflict it became evident that there could be no judge between them except the whole community of the church itself. In practice, the members of the church had to choose sides as conscience or interest dictated. In theory, at least two major authors of the mid fifteenth century, Panormitanus and Turrecremata (one a conciliarist, the other a papalist), realized that in case of fundamental conflict between the teaching of a pope and that of a council the issue could not be settled simply by attributing a greater authority to one side or the other. The church would have to follow the view that was best supported 'by reason and authorities', as Turrecremata put it. The argument seems to grow immediately out of the confused ecclesiastical politics of the 1440s. But in fact, as was so often the case, the fifteenth-century authors were also influenced by a twelfth-century canonist. Huguccio had considered this question, about 1190. 'Look', he wrote, 'A council is assembled from the whole church. Doubt arises. The pope alone renders one decision, all the others another. Which is to be preferred to which?' Huguccio held that an iniquitous decision from either side was to be rejected. If neither decision was clearly iniquitous, either could be chosen. 'They may be considered equal', he explained, 'since on one side is greater authority, on the other greater numbers.'[35]

Let us return to Gerson for a moment. He formulated several positions which would be repeated by later political theorists (sometimes with overt reference to conciliar thought). The authority latent in a community was not extinguished by a breakdown of its central government; rather the community could constitute a representative body to restore a universally accepted regime. Moreover, if a community was not a mere mass of individuals but was composed of members ordered in various degrees, then an assembly that adequately represented it would necessarily reflect in its composition various types of regimes. Such an assembly could be described in the language of medieval corporative associations or in Aristotelian language as a form of mixed constitution. There was, however, a major incoherence in Gerson's thought. His argument led to the paradox that a general council could exercise the papal authority against a person who was actually pope at the time the council acted. A similar paradox arose in the secular constitutional thought of the seventeenth century, and then it stimulated further reflections - with which we can end our investigation of these problems - on the structure of a complex government and on the relationship between such a government and

[35]   On the views of Panormitanus, Turrecremata, and Huguccio see my ' "Only the Truth has Authority": The Problem of "Reception" in the Decretists and in Johannes de Turrecremata', in K. Pennington and R. Somerville (eds.), *Law, Church and Society. Essays in Honor of Stephan Kuttner* (Philadelphia, 1977), pp. 69-96.

the community it represented. George Lawson defined the paradox starkly as it arose in England in the 1640s. 'Parliament declared they fought for King and Parliament . . . yet it fell out that the person who was King was Conquered . . . and put to death.'[36]

GEORGE LAWSON AND THE CIVIL WAR

Lawson is an attractive figure, a sensitive, sensible man of eirenic temperament, writing in an age of bitter sectarian animosities. To use his own words, he lived in 'sad and woful' times, in a land where legitimate civil government had collapsed, 'kept together rather by the sword of an army'. But, amid all this, Lawson could still write, 'God never did, Man never can give any power to be unjust', and again, 'all Communities, spiritual and temporal are grounded upon that Commandment of God, *Love thy Neighbour as thyself*.[37]

The circumstances of the 1650s made Lawson sharply aware of the relationship between theories of ecclesiastical and civil government. He began his *Politia sacra et civilis* with the remark, 'I easily understood that the Subject of our Differences was, not only the State but the Church'; and this initial observation determined the whole subsequent shape of his work. Lawson presented first a section on the right ordering of the state, then a section on the church, then another on the state and another on the church, and so on through the whole course of the book, developing in the parallel chapters symmetrical theories of civil and ecclesiastical authority. He discerned 'Rules of Government in general' that were the same in church and state, and he held that they could be derived from reason and nature or more easily from 'that Book of books, we call the holy Scriptures'.[38]

Given this whole style of thought, it is interesting that Lawson has attracted the attention of modern scholars principally for his supposed influence on John Locke, the paragon of Enlightenment rationalism; and indeed if Lawson ever finds a permanent niche in the standard histories of political theory it will probably be as a precursor of Locke. One finds essentially similar ideas in both authors. Thus Lawson, like Locke, distinguished clearly between government and community, between the right to rule and the right to institute rulers, between dissolution of a government and dissolution of a people. Such ideas were not entirely novel; certain forms of conciliar ecclesiology had developed along similar lines as we have seen, and Lawson knew something of conciliar thought. (He referred - not unsympathetically - to the views of Gerson and Nicholas

---

[36] G. Lawson, *Politia sacra et civilis*, 2nd edn (London, 1689), p. 94.
[37] *Politia*, pp. 97, 47; cf. p. 136, 'Civil government, being grounded upon the eternal moral Law, *Love thy Neighbour as thy self* . . .'
[38] *Politia*, pp. A2, 2, 452.

of Cues and Peter d'Ailly.)[39] Indeed, from our point of view Lawson's work may seem as much a finale as a prelude, an orchestration of already familiar themes; his *Politia sacra et civilis* is filled with elements of thought that we have encountered in previous writings on law, politics, and ecclesiology, now blended together in a new synthesis.[40]

The theoretical problem Lawson faced, to put the matter in very abstract terms, was that none of the conceptual apparatus available - neither the language of mixed constitution nor of corporation law (nor indeed of classical republicanism) - provided a solution for the problem of conflict between the different parts of a complex government. And Lawson had to deal with just such a conflict in real life. To cope with it, he used a vocabulary borrowed directly from Christopher Besold, who had developed a theory of double sovereignty in which 'personal majesty' was attributed to the ruler, 'real majesty' to the people. Lawson, however, went considerably beyond Besold in his development of both concepts.

In Lawson's work, both community and government were conceived of as corporate bodies deriving their respective authorities from consent. (Ideas first formulated as technical juristic abstractions had become so assimilated into common discourse that they could now be used routinely in political theory even by authors who were not lawyers.) Lawson maintained that a mere multitude of separate persons was not competent to institute a civil government; nor could a multitude of individual Christians institute a government for the church. First a community - either civil or ecclesiastical - had to be established; and this could be achieved only by voluntary association of the members (though they acted in accordance with man's natural social instinct and with God's all-embracing purpose). The community thus created formed a single corporate entity, 'one person morally considered' or, as Lawson put it in another work, 'one person moral by fiction of the law . . . as the Civilians express themselves'.[41]

Within the community members enjoyed rights of property (by natural law) and liberty and equality (in the sense that no external superior was set over them except God). At first the community had no government ('personal majesty') but it had an inherent right to institute government, to 'model a Commonwealth', and this was what Lawson understood by 'real majesty'. Personal majesty could be forfeited - 'it's no inseparable adjunct to any person'. But real majesty was inalienable. It inhered in a community before the establishment of a government, dur-

[39]   p. 295, citing Lancelot Andrewes. Cf. pp. 261, 264, 303, 'This is no Popery nor do the present Popes and the church of *Rome* like it.' Lawson, however, thought that the assembly of a council to rule the whole church was simply impracticable.
[40]   They will be easily recognizable; it seems superfluous to heap up countless cross-references to earlier works.
[41]   *Politia*, pp. 16-23, 36. See also *An Examination of the Political Part of Mr Hobbes His Leviathan* (London, 1657), p. 21.

ing a government's existence, and after a government's dissolution; it included also a power to 'alter the Form of the Government' or to remove a regime that had grown tyrannical. Actual powers of rulership could be exercised only by an established government but the government's personal majesty was always dependent on the real majesty of the community. 'Real is in the Community and is greater than Personal.'⁴²

This real majesty inhered in civil communities by natural law, and was conferred on the church by those now familiar words of Jesus at Matthew 18.17, 'Go tell it to the church.'⁴³ ('That's the only place for the Institution and no other', wrote Lawson.) Lawson was particularly insistent that a community capable of forming a commonwealth could come into existence only by free consent of the members. He held that consent, 'grounded upon Love and Good Affection', was God's way of working through man. 'But that whereby God is the immediate cause of Society is voluntary consent, to which he inclines their hearts.' Lawson noted that government had utilitarian ends; its purpose was to secure 'the peace and happiness of a community'; but he added at once that 'Love is the true cause of all association.' This is reminiscent of Althusius (whose work Lawson knew); but Lawson realized more clearly than his predecessor that, in basing a political theory on such premises, he was putting forward a distinctively theological doctrine. 'Politiks both civil and Ecclesiastical belong unto Theology, and are but a branch of the same.'⁴⁴

Lawson also differed from Althusius in distinguishing more sharply between the formation of a community and the constituting of a government. For him (as for Gerson) a community without government was 'like a matter without form'. The establishing of government required 'another consent - distinct and really different' from the consent that formed the community. Through this consent the government acquired 'not meerly a power to teach and direct . . . but to bind'. In a variation on the old language about 'wisdom and power' Lawson wrote that the exercise of sovereignty was 'an act of the Will' that 'presupposeth some act of the Understanding'.⁴⁵

The community could establish any form of government it chose, but when ruling power was conferred on more than one person (as in an aristocracy or a mixed constitution) the 'Polyarchal Sovereign' was considered 'as one person morally'. Lawson held that, although the acts of sovereignty could be differentiated as legislative, judicial, or executive, sovereignty itself could not be divided up so that one part was given to one person, another part to another. Personal majesty inhered in a single person or in a corporate group that formed one 'moral person'.⁴⁶ Similarly real majesty, the permanent power to institute a government or

---

⁴² *Politia*, pp. 27, 54-9, 91.   ⁴⁵ pp. 46, 36, 67, 51.
⁴³ pp. 58, 271.   ⁴⁶ pp. 66-71.
⁴⁴ pp. 16, 23, 47, 48.

replace it or change its form, inhered in the people not as a mere crowd of individual subjects but as a formed community.

These considerations shaped Lawson's approach to the English constitutional crisis of the 1640s. In England, he held, real majesty inhered in the whole people, personal majesty in a parliament 'consisting of King, Peers, and Commons jointly'. England was thus not a pure monarchy but a 'mixt state'. Also, since the king was himself an intrinsic part of parliament, he could not be greater than parliament. Quoting Sir Roger Owen, Lawson noted that the king was 'not above the Parliament because he cannot be above himself' and that 'together with them he was greater than himself'.[47] But it did not follow from this that the members of parliament, separated from the king, were greater than he. Lawson was dealing here with the same issue that we encountered in Gerson's ecclesiology. In the earlier discussions, the radical conciliarists had advocated a sort of unworkable ecclesiastical republicanism in which the members of a general council always prevailed over its head, while the more moderate ones took refuge in ambiguities or fell into inconsistencies. Lawson attacked the problem head on. For him, sovereignty inhered 'in the whole assembly as one body . . . a Representative of the whole Nation'. It followed that, when the king and the two houses of parliament fell into irreconcilable conflict, the framework of government was dissolved.[48] Earlier writers had often noted that an individual ruler could strip himself of sovereign power by his own actions; Lawson perceived more clearly than his predecessors that the same argument could apply to a whole complex government; and he pursued the implications of the argument more systematically.

In such circumstances (which had actually arisen in England) authority remained with the whole people. Although they had an obligation to support the more just cause in the Civil War 'according to the Laws of God' they were freed from political allegiance to any existing human government. But the whole point of the argument was that they were not freed from obligation to the community. 'Allegiance due to the Community of England did continue', Lawson wrote. Hence the community retained a right (and a duty) to institute a new government for itself. In trying to define more precisely where this right of the community resided, Lawson fell back on the old language of the canonists. Throughout the 'Bloody distractions' of the Civil War, he held, there had always persisted a sounder part (*sanior pars*) of the community; the right to re-institute government remained with this part or with its weightier portion acting on behalf of the whole community - '*in parte saniore, aut in parte hujus partis valentiore*'.[49]

To sum up: Lawson denied that the members of parliament could

[47] pp. 148, 161, 163, 162, 76.
[48] pp. 164, 371.
[49] pp. 371, 383.

assert a superior right over the king, but he acknowledged that the whole community could assert a superior right over any government. One might say that he relied implicitly on the complex model of corporations in considering the structure of the government, on the simple model in considering the structure of the state.

In considering the best form of government, Lawson expressed a conventional preference for a mixed constitution. Here again he restated an argument we have encountered in earlier ecclesiology, the view that a government reflecting the structure of an ordered community must necessarily include a mixture of regimes. Lawson discussed in turn the simple forms of rulership - monarchy, aristocracy, and democracy - finding fault with each. Then he turned to mixed government. He defined this system as 'a Free State, a popular State', in which 'the whole Power is wholly in the whole'. Lawson considered this 'the best, most just, and the wisest' form of government. He insisted that the system he advocated was not mere democracy, which indeed he regarded as the 'least and basest' of the simple forms.[50] He argued rather that in any community, even before government was constituted by consent, different classes would exist. Besides simple free men, there were others more eminent 'by reason of their Descent, Estates, Parts, Noble Acts', and then others again who were super-eminent, and among these there might be one outstanding man. When governing power resided 'wholly in the whole' it did not belong simply to the lower orders but to all these classes, who would contribute to government according to their quality in a representative body. Such a government would necessarily be a mixture of aristocracy and democracy, and perhaps of monarchy, aristocracy, and democracy, as in England.[51]

Lawson used similar patterns of argument in discussing the right form of government for the church. The power of the keys, he wrote, inhered in the church 'after the manner of a free State or Polity'; and, in the church too, along with simple Christians there were some members more eminent in wisdom and grace, fit to be leaders. Lawson turned to the example of ancient Israel in arguing that a church, like a nation, could best be governed by an assembly representing the whole people, and again produced an odd conjunction of Judaic and Anglo-Saxon precedents. 'Israel met in their Representative . . . As our State hath its *Wittena Gemot*, the Parliament . . . so a National Church may have a general Assembly to represent the whole.'[52] But, although he repeated the now stereotyped praise for the Mosaic constitution of the Old Testament, Lawson relied mainly on New Testament texts in discussing the constitution of the church. When Christ spoke the crucial words of institution at Matthew 18.17, Lawson explained, he did not say 'Go tell it to Peter'

[50] pp. 138-46, 82.
[51] pp. 25, 131-2.
[52] pp. 263, 43, 258, 339.

and establish a monarchy; nor did he say 'Go tell it to the apostles' and establish an aristocracy; nor did he say 'Go tell it to the people' and establish a democracy. He said 'Go tell it to the church' - and the church could include all these forms. Lawson thought that the elders and presbyters formed an aristocratic element in the church and the consent of the people a democratic element. He reserved the monarchical role for Christ.

Lawson's scriptural exegesis was evidently influenced by the categories of secular political theory; but his political theory - although in many ways so similar to Locke's - was also a kind of secularized ecclesiology, constantly deploying (and developing in new ways) ideas that we have encountered in earlier theories of church structure. Let us consider one last text. Although Lawson did not regard Christ's words to Peter at Matthew 16.19 ('I will give thee the keys of the kingdom of heaven') as constitutive of governing power in the church, he offered a fascinating comment on the various interpretations of the text that were current by the middle of the seventeenth century.

Many and different are the interpretations of this place, as given by Writers, both Ancient and Modern, Popish and Protestant . . . Some will have . . . *Peter* as a monarch . . . Some will have *Peter* here considered as the mouth and representative of the Apostles, and in them of all Aristocratical Bishops . . . Some will have him to represent . . . the Church itself . . . so that from this pronoun THEE we have Chymical extractions of all sorts of Governments, Ecclesiastical, pure and mixt, Monarchical, Aristocratical, Democratical . . .[53]

'Chymical extractions of . . . Governments'. It is an interesting image to find in an English author writing just a few years before the founding of the Royal Society in London.

Lawson's words can provide a fitting conclusion for a discussion on the interplay between secular and religious constitutional thought. They also point to a task for future scholarship; for we have not yet analyzed adequately those 'Chymical extractions of all sorts of Governments' that were derived from Christ's words to Peter. Indeed, after all the writing of the past forty years on canonistic theories of government in church and state, perhaps the work that could be most helpful now in this whole area of research would be a systematic study on the ecclesiastical theories of a mixed constitution.

[53] pp. 264-5.

VI

Conclusion

The first emergence of sophisticated, consciously held constitutional doctrines from the chaos of the early medieval world was a little like the emergence of life and consciousness itself - as the scientists currently tell the story - from the primeval ocean of inanimate matter. In the old medieval ocean of folk customs unthinkingly observed and religious practices unreflectively pursued, molecules of conscious questioning thought appeared, usually at points where elements of religious and secular thought coalesced. Eventually the molecules came together in complex aggregates, like living organisms capable of reproducing themselves in the minds of men. *Capable* of reproducing themselves! But at that point all the problems of selection and adaptation and survival arise.

Even when all the evident gaps in our knowledge have been filled in, we shall still no doubt have our problems in understanding the whole evolution of Western constitutional thought - the nature of its origins and the reasons for its survival. The problems are implied in a crisp sentence of Christopher Hill: 'The seventeenth is the decisive century of English history, the epoch in which the Middle Ages ended.'[1] The difficulty here is that, in the realm of constitutional theory, nothing of the sort happened. During the Middle Ages an unusual structure of constitutional thought arose. Its exponents were preoccupied with consent, legitimacy, community rights, and, beyond these generalities, with rather technical problems concerning the relationship between central and local government, representation, rights of resistance, collegiate sovereignty, the distribution of authority within a complex collegiate sovereign. Such themes are common to medieval law, to fifteenth-century conciliarism, and to seventeenth-century constitutional theory. The resemblances are too striking to be mere coincidences; but merely to call attention to resemblances is not to explain the whole phenomenon. The recurrence of similar patterns of thought in different historical environments is itself the problem that needs elucidating.

A common approach to the problem, when it is considered at all, is to trace the influence of one thinker on another down the course of the centuries. This way of studying the ancestry of ideas can be interesting

[1] C. Hill, *God's Englishman* (New York, 1970), p. 15.

and rewarding. It is soothing, perhaps, to reflect that George Lawson knew the views of Peter d'Ailly, and d'Ailly used John of Paris, and John of Paris quoted Johannes Teutonicus, and Johannes Teutonicus relied extensively on Huguccio - and Huguccio was a twelfth-century canonist who commented on Gratian's *Decretum*. But this approach has its limitations. Some seventeenth-century authors quoted in support of their views late medieval writings like those of the conciliarists (who in turn transmitted earlier medieval traditions); others preferred not to do so. Often we find notable resemblances of thought and expression between a later author and a much earlier one when there is no evident link between them. Even in these cases though, it may seem that a simple explanation will suffice. Some ancient texts never lost their authority. Patterns of thought and language were often repeated because, although the range of references expanded greatly, constitutional theorists turned back most often to the same basic source materials - Aristotle, the Old and New Testaments, civil and canon law. Similar ideas often have a common ancestry even when there is no direct filiation between them.

At this point, however, a difficulty of interpretation can arise. The use of ancient sources by seventeenth-century authors may sometimes obscure the actual medieval basis of their thought. We can avoid being misled about this if we acquire a little sensitivity to the language of seventeenth-century political discourse. Sometimes it can tell us more than a particular author intended. Humanist and religious reformers of the early modern period often felt a sense of alienation from their immediate past, a need to distance themselves from it, and a corresponding enthusiasm for the virtues of classical antiquity or for the primitive purity of the early church. Not infrequently they convinced themselves that they had made a new beginning by reviving the values of the ancient world (whether Christian or classical), when what they were really reviving was some aspect of a medieval tradition which for a time had seemed outworn. The more radical Protestant reformers, for instance, believed that they could turn their backs on the whole history of the church for a thousand years; and yet, in studying ecclesiology, the beginning of wisdom is an awareness that the medieval church was the mother of all the Western churches. It is the same with secular constitutional theory. The point here is that, even when seventeenth-century writers chose not to cite medieval authorities, the language of their discourse (and the thought it conveyed) had often been shaped by medieval usage. This applies not least to their ways of deploying texts from Scripture or classical antiquity. Specifically, for instance, when an early modern author cited Matthew 18.17 as an argument for popular government or *Cod.* 5.59.5 (*Quod omnes tangit*) as an argument for political consent, he was attributing to the ancient texts meanings that had been imprinted on them by medieval experience.

This is especially apparent in references to the idea of a mixed constitution. In their discussions on this theme seventeenth-century authors very seldom quoted medieval sources; they preferred to rely on some respected classical writer - Aristotle or Polybius or Cicero perhaps - as the authority for their views. (George Lawson did not cite Gerson - or any conciliarist - in discussing mixed government though he did cite Dionysius of Halicarnassus.) But what the early modern authors commonly had in mind was a collegiate sovereign of king, lords, and commons, or pope, cardinals, and general council presiding as a representative assembly over a national state or a universal church. Such arrangements have little in common with the ancient polis. Rather evidently, both the institutions and the ideas which explained their functioning were rooted in a medieval tradition of practice and theory. But often the existence of such a tradition would not be apparent if we read only the later works that are its end products. Seventeenth-century writers were often thinking medieval thoughts even when they clothed them in classical dress.

This still leaves us with a major problem. So far we have considered only the ways in which one can trace the transmission of medieval thought to the modern world. The more serious questions remain. Why did the medieval ideas persist? Why did they continue to prove meaningful and useful? Even when we can explain the process of transmission in the simplest fashion - even when we can construct a neat little chain of texts leading all the way from the twelfth century to the seventeenth (and this is indeed often possible) - we have still not answered, we have not even addressed, these more difficult questions.

The period we have been discussing was one of significant change in almost every sphere of activity. Art changed, and architecture - and artillery. Science changed, and society. New theologies appeared, and new ways of economic life. Astronomers discovered a new heaven and explorers a New World. But through all this, improbably, patterns of constitutional theory persisted that had originally grown out of the structure of medieval society and the encounter of medieval Christian intellectuals with the secular thought of Greece and Rome. It follows that the task of a scholar is not merely to pursue threads of influence from author to author down through the centuries. The further, more complex task for historians will be to understand what elements of continuity existed in political and religious life (during a period of such incessant change) which might explain the survival of medieval ways of thought into the modern era.

Here I can offer only the briefest suggestions. Although so much changed, some problems persisted. The tensions between central and local government never ceased to exist and continued to offer difficulties of theory and practice. Seventeenth-century thinkers had to reconcile as best they could the claims of court and country, king and nobles, emperor and princes, pope and bishops, general assembly and local presbytery. Two issues arose - the guaranteeing of local rights through fundamental constitutional law, and the participation of local representatives in shaping the decisions of central government. The example of the classical polis was again of little relevance here; but medieval authors had already adapted elements of ancient thought to cope with similar problems of their own society; and so their ideas remained useful and applicable in the new age.

Similarly, the medieval habit of basing constitutional doctrines on theories of corporation structure persisted because it remained pertinent to the social and religious life of the early modern world. During the sixteenth and seventeenth centuries, in many parts of Europe, men were again coming together to form new kinds of communities and - overtly or tacitly - were applying the principles of such associations to the construction of generalized theories of government. In the secular sphere, on a very mundane level, we have to study the private charters of commercial enterprises in order to understand some aspects of early American constitutional thought (just as we have to study the private law of corporations in order to understand some forms of medieval constitutional doctrine). In the religious sphere, innumerable new congregations were formed by voluntary covenant, by free deliberate association of the members, and the experience profoundly influenced reflections on government in general. It ensured that community always offered an alternative to hierarchy as a model of right order in human societies. John Robinson, discussing church governance, declared, 'We must be with one another, not over one another. There must be consociation, not subordination.' And, however much scholars disagree about the political views of Calvin himself, no one imagines that we can understand the development of Calvinist political theory in isolation from such tenets of Calvinist ecclesiology.

This is the central point for us. The old tensions and interactions between church and state never died away. Ecclesiology and secular constitutional thought continued to influence one another. We have noticed that a theory of the autonomous secular state emerged earlier than is sometimes supposed; but we need to remember also that, alongside it, a more primitive way of thinking always persisted. Throughout our period, constitutional theorists were in the habit - often unconsciously, though consciously enough in the case of some Calvinists - of regarding the political community as also an ecclesial community, a people of God. Stephen Langton, in the thirteenth century, held that royal power was derived from the church understood as the congregation of the faithful, the whole Christian community.[2] In the fourteenth century the somewhat eccentric author of *A Mirror for Magistrates* observed that parliament had met in England ever since the days of King Alfred for 'the

[2] See p. 41.

guidance of the people of God, how the fold should keep themselves from sin'.[3] A fifteenth-century Speaker of the House of Commons compared the celebration of a parliament with the celebration of a Mass, and a sixteenth-century spokesman averred that the Holy Ghost was as surely present in an English parliament as in any church council. For John Milton, in the seventeenth century, 'the church might be called a commonwealth and the whole commonwealth a church'.[4] This attitude helps to explain the persistent appeal of ancient Israel - both a nation and a church - as a model of ideal government; it also ensured that religious and secular ideas on government would not cease to interact with one another. Of course theologians and political thinkers were not incapable of distinguishing conceptually between the two spheres. John Robinson of Massachusetts, whom we first mentioned as a supporter of mixed government in the church, observed cautiously in another context that principles of church authority did not necessarily apply to civil polities;[5] but in practice, both in New England and in old England, it proved impossible to keep ecclesiology and political theory in watertight compartments. They kept spilling over into one another.

This was especially important for the development of the doctrine of consent. The old medieval conflict of church and state had tended to desacralize kingship; but it did not desanctify the community. The church itself was always conceived of as a free society united by the voluntary consent of the members. No one disagreed in principle with Nicholas of Cues' doctrine that Christ would accept only a willing believer; and, when the principle seemed to be collapsing under a weight of contrary practice at the end of the Middle Ages, it was passionately reaffirmed by Protestant theologians. One of them wrote, 'The consent of a believer is an essential part of belief.' When men moved by such convictions sought an alternative to the resurgent doctrine of the divine right of kings, they could readily take up the medieval teaching, always conveniently at hand, that consent was the basis of all legitimate government, and make it their own.

At the same time, the mutual persecutions of the age led both Catholic and Protestant writers - depending on who was being persecuted at a particular time and place - to reformulate medieval doctrines of resistance to unjust rulers and of limited constitutional government. This was

---

[3]   B. Wilkinson, *Studies in the Constitutional History of the Thirteenth and Fourteenth Centuries* (Manchester, 1937), p. 252. For the fifteenth-century and sixteenth-century comments see Kantorowicz, *King's Two Bodies*, p. 227, and G. R. Elton, *Reform and Renewal* (Cambridge, 1973), p. 67.

[4]   Mary A. Radzinowicz, *Toward Samson Agonistes* (Princeton, 1978), p. 151.

[5]   John Robinson, *Works*, II, 143. Similarly some conciliarists, anxious not to alienate royal support, insisted that their constitutionalist doctrines applied only in the ecclesiastical sphere. Bellarmine, on the other hand, preferred pure monarchy in the church and constitutional restraints in the state. But much of the time it seemed simpler to suppose that God would want his people to be governed in the same way, whether they were organized as a church or a state.

indeed the principal legacy that Reformation theorists transmitted to later political thought. We need not be oversentimental about their motives. They were not 'fighting to bring about our modern world'. As Figgis explained, 'What they desired was not liberty or tolerance but independence and domination.' This observation is certainly true; but possibly it does not convey quite the whole truth. Perhaps we can carry the argument just a little further.

Once we have abandoned any notion of an 'inevitable principle of progress' at work in history it may seem that the whole tradition of Western constitutional thought - both its origin and persistence - can be explained only as the result of a random play of contingent circumstances. (An odd tension in medieval society was accidently perpetuated by a religious upheaval at the end of the Middle Ages.) And, when we consider the self-interest of the religious groups who mainly nurtured constitutional ideas, mere cynicism may seem the only appropriate response. Yet a modern scholar may still experience moments of doubt - embarrassing though it is for him to have intellectual doubts about his own cynicism - when it seems that some further understanding might be possible.

Perhaps, after all, sectarian self-interest does not explain every aspect of the tradition we have explored. I recall our twelfth-century canonist Gratian, who thought he could build a whole convoluted structure of law on the simple Golden Rule, 'Do unto others as you would have them do unto you'; and Gerson, who believed in the 'infinite creativeness' of the Christian community; and Nicholas of Cues, who dreamed of universal consensus and concord; and Althusius, who was led to a doctrine of consent by a conviction that no man was valueless in the eyes of God; and George Lawson, who in an age of sectarian hatreds could still affirm that all human association was based on love. All this suggests one final tentative reflection. Perhaps, after all, it was not only the circumstances in which our protagonists were placed that determined the outcome of their thought, but in part too the very nature of the religious tradition to which they appealed. Certainly Christian teaching did not lead on inevitably to theories of constitutional government; that development was at best a possibility, a potentiality. Christian tradition, in different circumstances, could easily lead to different results, to various forms of absolutism. It was only through hard, bitter specific experiences from the twelfth century onward that Western man came to perceive how the old truths of his religion could serve as foundations for a new constitutional order. But the perception itself, however gained, may still prove of enduring value if, after all, our tradition should persist as something more than a mere aberration in the general story of mankind.

Select bibliography

This list contains secondary literature cited in notes to the text together with suggestions for further reading. It includes some general works on political theory and some more specialized studies dealing with particular persons and themes that are touched on in the lectures.

Alberigo, G. *Cardinalato e collegialità; studi sull' ecclesiologia tra l'XI e il XIV secolo.* Florence, 1969

Allen, J. W. *English Political Thought 1603-1660.* London, 1938
  A History of Political Thought in the Sixteenth Century. London, 1960

Anderson, Perry. *Lineages of the Absolutist State.* London, 1974

Baldwin, J. W. *Masters, Princes and Merchants.* 2 vols. Princeton, 1970

Barker, E. *The Dominican Order and Convocation.* Oxford, 1913

Baron, Hans. *The Crisis of the Italian Renaissance: Civic Humanism and Republican Liberty in an Age of Classicism and Tyranny.* 2 vols. Princeton, 1955
  'Calvinist Republicanism and its Historical Roots', *Church History,* 8 (1939), 30-42

Bayley, C. C. 'Pivotal Concepts in the Political Philosophy of William of Ockham', *Journal of the History of Ideas,* 10 (1949), 199-218

Bendix, R. *Kings or People: Power and the Mandate to Rule.* Berkeley-Los Angeles, 1978

Benert, Richard R. 'Lutheran Resistance Theory and the Imperial Constitution', *Il Pensiero Politico,* 6 (1973), 17-36

Black, Antony. *Monarchy and Community: Political Ideas in the Later Conciliar Controversy 1430-1450.* Cambridge, 1970
  Council and Commune: The Conciliar Movement and the Fifteenth-Century Heritage. London, 1979

Bowe, G. *The Origin of Political Authority.* Dublin, 1955

Bowle, John. *Hobbes and his Critics: A Study in Seventeenth-Century Constitutionalism.* London, 1951

Bowsma, W. 'Gallicanism and the Nature of Christendom', in A. Molho (ed.), *Renaissance Studies in Honor of Hans Baron,* 811-30. De Kalb, 1971

Buisson, Ludwig. *Potestas und Caritas. Die päpstliche Gewalt im Spätmittelalter.* Cologne, 1958

Burns, J. H. 'The Political Ideas of George Buchanan', *The Scottish Historical Review,* 30 (1951), 60-8

Butterfield, Herbert. *The Whig Interpretation of History.* London, 1931

Calasso, Francesco. *I Glossatori e la teoria della sovranità.* 3rd edn. Milan, 1957

Cam, Helen. *Liberties and Communities in Medieval England.* Cambridge, 1944

Canning, J. P. 'The Corporation in the Political Thought of the Jurists of the Thirteenth and Fourteenth Centuries', *History of Political Theory*, 1 (1980), 9-32

Carlyle, R. W. and A. J. *A History of Mediaeval Political Theory in the West.* 6 vols. Edinburgh-London, 1903-36

Carney, F. S. Introduction to *The Politics of Johannes Althusius.* Boston, 1964

Chrimes, S. B. *English Constitutional Ideas in the Fifteenth Century.* Cambridge, 1936

Chroust, Anton-Hermann. 'The Corporate Idea and the Body Politic in the Middle Ages', *Review of Politics*, 9 (1947), 423-52

Church, William F. *Constitutional Thought in Sixteenth-Century France.* Cambridge, Mass., 1941

Clarke, Maude V. *Medieval Representation and Consent.* London, 1936

Congar, Yves M.-J. 'Quod omnes tangit ab omnibus tractari et approbari debet', *Revue historique de droit français et étranger*, 4e sér., 36 (1958), 210-59

'Aspects ecclésiologiques de la querelle entre mendiants et séculiers dans la seconde moitié du XIIIe siècle et le début du XIVe', *Archives d'histoire doctrinale et littéraire du moyen âge*, 36 (1961), 35-151

Cortese, Ennio. *La norma guiridica. Spunti teorici nel diritto commune classico.* 2 vols. Milan, 1962-4.

Costa, Pietro. *Iurisdictio. Semantica del potere politico nella pubblicistica medievale.* Milan, 1969

Davis, S. Rufus. *The Federal Principle: A Journey Through Time in Quest of a Meaning.* Berkeley-Los Angeles, 1978

Dufeil, M. M. *Guillaume de Saint-Amour et la polémique universitaire parisienne, 1250-1259.* Paris, 1972

Dunn, John. 'Consent in the Political Theory of John Locke', *The Historical Journal*, 10 (1967), 153-82

Eccleshall, R. *Order and Reason in Politics. Theories of Absolute and Limited Monarchy in Early Modern England.* Oxford, 1978

Edwards, J. G. 'The *Plena Potestas* of English Parliamentary Representatives', in *Oxford Essays in Medieval History Presented to H. E. Salter.* Oxford, 1934

Elarzar, D. J. 'Federalism', in *International Encyclopedia of the Social Sciences*, V, 353-67. New York, 1968

Elton, G. R. *Reform and Renewal: Thomas Cromwell and the Commonweal.* Cambridge, 1973

Ercole, F. *Da Bartolo all' Althusio.* Florence, 1932

Eschmann, I. Th. 'A Thomistic Glossary on the Principle of the Preëminence of a Common Good', *Mediaeval Studies*, 5 (1943), 123-65

Fernandez Rios, M. 'El primado del Romano pontifice nel pensamiento de Huguccio de Pisa decretista', *Compostellanum*, 6 (1961), 47-97; 7 (1962), 97-149; 8 (1963), 65-99; 11 (1966), 29-67

Figgis, J. N. *The Divine Right of Kings.* 2nd edn. Cambridge, 1914

Political Thought from Gerson to Grotius, 1414-1625. Seven Studies, with an Introduction by Garrett Mattingly. New York, 1960

Franklin, J. H. *Constitutionalism and Resistance in the Sixteenth Century.* New York, 1969

Jean Bodin and the Rise of Absolutist Theory. Cambridge, 1973

John Locke and the Theory of Sovereignty. Cambridge, 1978

Friedrich, C. J. Introduction to *Politica methodica digesta of Johannes Althusius.* Cambridge, Mass., 1932

Constitutional Reason of State. Providence, 1957

Gewirth, Alan. *Marsilius of Padua. The Defender of the Peace.* 2 vols. New York, 1951-6

Gierke, Otto. *Das deutsche Genossenschaftsrecht.* 4 vols. Berlin, 1868-1914

Political Theories of the Middle Ages. Trans. by F. W. Maitland. Cambridge, 1900

The Development of Political Theory. Trans. by B. Freyd. New York, 1930

Natural Law and the Theory of Society, 1500-1800. Trans. by E. Barker. Cambridge, 1934

Giesey, R. 'Medieval Jurisprudence in Bodin's Concept of Sovereignty', in Horst Denzer (ed.), *Jean Bodin: Proceedings of the International Conference on Bodin in Munich,* 167-86. Munich, 1973

Gilby, T. *Principality and Polity. Aquinas and the Rise of State Theory in the West.* New York, 1958

Gillet, P. *La personnalité juridique en droit ecclésiastique.* Malines, 1927

Gillmann, F. 'Richardus Anglicus als Glossator der Compilatio I', *Archiv für katholisches Kirchenrecht,* 107 (1927), 575-655

Gilmore, Myron P. *Argument from Roman Law in Political Thought, 1200-1600.* Cambridge, Mass., 1941

Gough, J. W. *The Social Contract: A Critical Study of its Development.* 2nd edn. Oxford, 1957

Gwyn, W. B. *The Meaning of the Separation of Powers.* New Orleans, 1965

Hackett, J. H. 'State of the Church: A Concept of the Medieval Canonists', *The Jurist,* 23 (1963), 259-90

Hamilton, Bernice. *Political Thought in Sixteenth-Century Spain: A Study of the Political Ideas of Vitoria, De Sota, Suarez, and Molina.* Oxford, 1963

Hanson, Donald W. *From Kingdom to Commonwealth. The Development of Civic Consciousness in English Political Thought.* Cambridge, Mass., 1970

Haskins, G. L. *Growth of English Representative Government.* Philadelphia, 1948

Hatch, N. O. *The Sacred Cause of Liberty.* New Haven, 1977

Heydte, F. A. Freiherr von. *Die Geburtsstunde des souveränen Staates.* Regensburg, 1952

Hill, C. *God's Englishman.* New York, 1970

Hintze, O. 'Weltgeschichtliche Bedingungen der Repraesentativverfassung', *Historiche Zeitschrift,* 143 (1930), 1-47

Hofmann, H. *Repraesentation: Studien zur Wort- und Begriffsgeschichte von der Antike bis ins 19. Jahrhundert.* Berlin, 1974

Janelle, Pierre. *Obedience in Church and State.* Cambridge, 1930

Kantorowicz, E. H. *The King's Two Bodies. A Study in Medieval Political Theology.* Princeton, 1957

Kelley, Donald R. *Foundations of Modern Historical Scholarship.* New York, 1970

Koch, J. *Durandus de S. Porciano, O. P.* Münster, 1927

Kölmel, W. *Wilhelm Ockham und seine kirchenpolitischen Schriften.* Essen, 1962

Kuttner, Stephan. *Repertorium der Kanonistik.* Città del Vaticano, 1937

Ladner, Gerhart B. 'Aspects of Mediaeval Thought on Church and State', *Review of Politics,* 9 (1947), 403-22

'The Concepts: Ecclesia, Christianitas, Plenitudo Potestatis', *Sacerdozio e regno da Gregorio VII a Bonifacio VIII.* Miscellanea Historiae Pontificiae, XVIII [Rome, 1954]

Lagarde, G. de. *La naissance de l'esprit laïque au déclin du moyen âge.* 6 vols. Rev. edn. Louvain-Paris, 1956-70

'Individualisme et corporatisme au moyen âge', *L'Organisation corporative du moyen âge á la fin de l'ancien régime (Etudes presentées à la Commission Internationale pour l'Histoire des Assemblées d'Etats, II).* Louvain, 1937

Laski, Harold J. 'Political Theory in the Later Middle Ages', in J. R. Tanner *et al.* (eds.), *The Cambridge Medieval History*, VIII, 620-45. 8 vols., Cambridge, 1911-36

Introduction to *A Defense of Liberty against Tyrants*. London, 1924

Leclerq, Jean. *Jean de Paris et l'ecclésiologie du XIIIe siècle*. Paris, 1942

Lewis, Ewart. *Medieval Political Ideas*. 2 vols. London, 1954

'Organic Tendencies in Medieval Political Thought', *American Political Science Review*, 37 (1938), 849-76

'Natural Law and Expediency in Medieval Political Theory', *Ethics*, 50 (1939-40), 144-63

'The "Positivism" of Marsiglio of Padua', *Speculum*, 38 (1963), 541-82

Lewy, Guenter. *Constitutionalism and Statecraft during the Golden Age of Spain: a Study of the Political Philosophy of Juan de Mariana, S. J.* Geneva, 1960

Lousse, E. 'Parlementairisme ou corporatisme? Les origines des assemblées d'états', *Revue historique de droit français et étranger*, 14 (1935), 683-706

Lovejoy, A. O. *The Great Chain of Being*. New York, 1960

Lubac, Henri de. *Corpus mysticum*. 2nd edn. Paris, 1949

Lucca, L. de. 'L'accettazione popolare della legge canonica nel pensiero di Graziano e dei sui interpreti', *Studia Gratiana*, 3 (1955), 193-276

McGrade, Arthur S. *The Political Thought of William of Ockham*. Cambridge, 1974

McIlwain, C. H. *Growth of Political Thought in the West*. New York, 1932

Constitutionalism: Ancient and Modern. Ithaca, 1940

Maclean, A. H. 'George Lawson and John Locke', *Cambridge Historical Journal*, 9 (1947), 68-87

McNeill, John T. 'The Democratic Element in Calvin's Thought', *Church History*, 18 (1949), 153-71

Marongiu, Antonio. *L'Istituto parlamentare in Italia dalle origini al 1500*. Milan, 1949

Mesnard, Pierre. *L'Essor de la philosophie politique au XVIe siècle*. Paris, 1936

Meyjes, G. H. M. Posthumus. *Jean Gerson, zijn kerkpolitiek en eccliosologie*. 's-Gravenhage, 1963

Michaud-Quantin, P. *Universitas. Expressions du mouvement communautaire dans le moyen-âge latin*. Paris, 1970

Mochi Onory, Sergio. *Fonti canonistiche dell'idea moderna dello stato*. Milan, 1951

Mogi, S. *The Problem of Federalism*. 2 vols. London, 1931

Morrall, John B. *Political Thought in Medieval Times*. 2nd edn. London, 1960

Gerson and the Great Schism. Manchester, 1960

Morris, Colin. *The Discovery of the Individual, 1060-1200*. New York, 1972

Morrison, Karl. *Tradition and Authority in the Western Church, 300-1140*. Princeton, 1969

Muldoon, J. *Popes, Lawyers, and Infidels: The Church and the Non-Christian World*. Philadelphia, 1979

Oakley, Francis. *The Political Thought of Pierre d'Ailly: the Voluntarist Tradition*. New Haven, Conn., 1964

'On the Road from Constance to 1688: the Political Thought of John Major and George Buchanan', *Journal of British Studies*, 2 (1962), 1-31

'Almain and Major: Conciliar Theory on the Eve of the Reformation', *American Historical Review*, 70 (1964-5), 673-90

'Figgis, Constance and the Divines of Paris', *American Historical Review*, 75 (1969-70), 368-86

Oberman, Heiko A. *The Harvest of Medieval Theology*. Cambridge, Mass., 1963

Forerunners of the Reformation. New York, 1966

Pascoe, L. B. *Jean Gerson: Principles of Church Reform*. Leiden, 1973
Pelikan, Jaroslav. *Spirit versus Structure: Luther and the Institutions of the Church*. London, 1968
Pennington, K. and R. Somerville (eds.). *Law, Church and Society. Essays in Honor of Stephan Kuttner*. Philadelphia, 1977
Piaget, J. *Behavior and Evolution*. New York, 1978
Pirenne, H. *Medieval Cities*. Princeton, 1952
Pocock, John G. H. *The Machiavellian Moment: Florentine Political Thought and the Atlantic Republican Tradition*. Princeton, 1975
Post, Gaines. *Studies in Medieval Legal Thought*. Princeton, 1964 [Collected essays]
Powicke, F. M. 'Reflections on the Medieval State', *Transactions of the Royal Historical Society*, 19 (1936), 1-18
Previté-Orton, C. W. Introduction to *The Defensor Pacis of Marsilius of Padua*. Cambridge, 1928
'Marsilius of Padua', *Proceedings of the British Academy*, 21 (1935), 137-83
Quillet, J. *Le défenseur de la paix*. Paris, 1968
Radzinowicz, Mary A. *Toward Samson Agonistes*. Princeton, 1978
Reibstein, E. *Johannes Althusius als Fortsetzer der Schule von Salamanca*. Karlsruhe, 1955
Riesenberg, Peter. *Inalienability of Sovereignty in Medieval Political Thought*. New York, 1956
Riley, P. 'How Coherent is the Social Contract Tradition?', *Journal of the History of Ideas*, 34 (1973), 543-62
Rivière, J. *Le problème de l'église et de l'état au temps de Phillippe le Bel*. Louvain-Paris, 1926
Roberti, M. 'Il *corpus mysticum* di S. Paolo nella storia della persona giuridica', in *Studi in Onore di E. Besta*, IV, 37-82. Milan, 1939
Roche, J. P. 'Constitutional Law', in *International Encyclopedia of the Social Sciences*, III, 300-17. New York, 1968
Sabine, George H. *A History of Political Theory*. 3rd edn. London, 1963
Sägmüller, J. B. *Die Thätigkeit und Stellung der Kardinäle bis Papst Bonifaz VIII*. Freiburg, 1896
Salmon, J. H. M. *The French Religious Wars in English Political Thought*. Oxford, 1959
Schochet, Gordon J. *Patriarchalism in Political Thought: The Authoritarian Family and Political Speculation and Attitudes Especially in Seventeenth-Century England*. Oxford, 1975
Schramm, P. 'Sacerdotium und Regnum im Austausch ihrer Vorrechte', *Studi Gregoriani*, 2 (1947), 403-57
Sigmund, Paul E. *Nicholas of Cusa and Medieval Political Thought*. Harvard, 1963
Sikes, J. G. 'John de Pouilly and Peter de la Palu', *English Historical Review*, 49 (1934), 219-40
Skinner, Quentin. *The Foundations of Modern Political Thought*. 2 vols. Cambridge, 1978
Smith, A. L. *Church and State in the Middle Ages*. Oxford, 1913
Stickler, Alfons M. 'Concerning the Political Theories of the Medieval Canonists', *Traditio*, 7 (1949-51), 450-63
'Sacerdotium et regnum nei decretisti e primi decretalisti', *Salesianum*, 15 (1953), 575-612
Strayer, J. R. *On the Medieval Origins of the Modern State*. Princeton, 1970
Medieval Statecraft and the Perspectives of History. Princeton, 1971 [Collected essays]

Strohl, H. 'Le droit à la résistance d'après les conceptions protestantes', *Revue d'histoire et de philosophie religieuses*, 10 (1930), 126-44

Tierney, Brian. *Foundations of the Conciliar Theory. The Contribution of the Medieval Canonists from Gratian to the Great Schism.* Cambridge, 1955

Origins of Papal Infallibility, 1150-1350. Leiden, 1972

Church Law and Constitutional Thought in the Middle Ages. London, 1979 [Collected essays]

Tuck, R. *Natural Rights Theories: Their Origin and Development.* Cambridge, 1979

Ullmann, Walter. *The Medieval Idea of Law as Represented by Lucas de Penna.* London, 1946

Medieval Papalism. London, 1949

Principles of Government and Politics in the Middle Ages. London, 1961

Law and Politics in the Middle Ages. London, 1975

Medieval Foundations of Renaissance Humanism. Ithaca, 1977

Van de Kerckhove, M. 'La notion de juridiction dans la doctrine des décrétistes et des premiers décrétalistes', *Etudes franciscaines,* 49 (1937), 420-55

Vile, M. J. C. *Constitutionalism and the Separation of Powers.* Oxford, 1967

Vinogradoff, P. *Roman Law in Medieval Europe.* 2nd edn, by F. de Zulueta. Oxford, 1929

Vooght, P. de. *Les pouvoirs du concile et l'autorité du pape.* Paris, 1965

Watanabe, Morimichi. *The Political Ideas of Nicholas of Cusa: With Special Reference to his 'De Concordantia Catholica'.* Geneva, 1963

Watt, J. A. 'The Early Medieval Canonists and the Formation of Conciliar Theory', *Irish Theological Quarterly,* 24 (1957), 13-31

'The Theory of Papal Monarchy in the Thirteenth Century: The Contribution of the Canonists', *Traditio,* 20 (1964), 179-317

John of Paris. On Royal and Papal Power. Toronto, 1971

'Hostiensis on *Per venerabilem:* The Role of the College of Cardinals', in B. Tierney and P. Linehan (eds.), *Authority and Power. Studies on Medieval Law and Government Presented to Walter Ullmann on his Seventieth Birthday,* 193-218. Cambridge, 1980

Weston, C. C. 'The Theory of Mixed Monarchy Under Charles I and After', *English Historical Review,* 75 (1960), 426-43

Wilkinson, B. *Studies in the Constitutional History of the Thirteenth and Fourteenth Centuries.* Manchester, 1937

Wilks, Michael J. *The Problem of Sovereignty in the Later Middle Ages.* Cambridge, 1963

Wood, Gordon S. *The Creation of the American Republic, 1776-1787.* Chapel Hill, 1969

Woodhouse, A. S. P. *Puritanism and Liberty.* London, 1938

Woolf, C. N. S. *Bartolus of Sassoferrato.* Cambridge, 1913

Wormuth, Francis D. *The Origins of Modern Constitutionalism.* New York, 1949

Zagorin, Perez. *A History of Political Thought in the English Revolution.* London, 1954

Zimmermann, H. *Papstabsetzungen des Mittelalters.* Graz, 1968